UNION

by

Tim Barrow

D1465109

Published by Playdead Press 2014

© Tim Barrow 2014

Tim Barrow has asserted his rights under the Copyright, Design and Patents Act, 1988, to be identified as the author of this work.

A CIP catalogue record for this book is available from the British Library.

ISBN 978-1-910067-10-9

Printed by BPUK

Playdead Press
www.playdeadpress.com

The first performance of *Union* took place at the Royal Lyceum Theatre Edinburgh on 20 March, 2014.

CAST

Josh Whitelaw	Allan Ramsay
Sally Reid	Grace
Liam Brennan	Duke of Queensberry/ Tea Salesman
Irene Allan	Queen Anne
Ifan Meredith	Daniel Defoe/Lord Halifax/ Sergeant
Andrew Vincent	Duke of Marlborough/ Duke of Hamilton
Keith Fleming	Macdonald/Robert Harley/ Lord Belhaven
Mark McDonnell	Earl of Seafield/William Congreve/ Master of House
Tony Cownie	Earl of Stair/Robert Walpole
Rebecca Palmer	Sarah Churchill/Favour

CREATIVE TEAM

Mark Thomson	Director
Tim Barrow	Writer
Andrzej Goulding	Designer/Video Artist
Chris Davey	Lighting Designer
Megan Baker	Costume Designer
Philip Pinsky	Composer/Sound Designer
Becky Palmer	Assistant Director
Heather Wilson	Deputy Stage Manager
Julia Dixon-Phillips	Assistant Stage Manager

CAST

JOSH WHITELAW
Allan Ramsay
Recent theatre appearances
Misery Guts, Macbeth, Tartuffe, The Cherry Orchard, They Shoot Horses Don't They, Romeo and Juliet, Jack and the Beanstalk (Royal Conservatoire of Scotland).
Television, film and radio
Wasteland 26 (Breaking Point Flix); *Outcast* (Fantastic Films/Makar Films).
Josh is currently studying at the Royal Conservatoire of Scotland and will graduate in Summer 2014.

SALLY REID
Grace
Royal Lyceum Theatre appearances
The Guid Sisters (co-production with National Theatre of Scotland); *Time and the Conways* (co-production with Dundee Rep).
Recent theatre appearances
Peter Panto & The Incredible Stinkerbell, Aganeza Scrooge (Tron Theatre); *Blithe Spirit* (Perth Rep); *A Satire of the Three Estates* (Historic Scotland); *An Appointment with the Wicker Man* (National Theatre of Scotland); *Days of Wine and Roses, Doubt* (Theatre Jezebel/Tron Theatre); *Smalltown* (Random Accomplice).
Television, film and radio
The Scot Squad (Comedy Unit/BBC); *Rab C. Nesbitt* (RDF

Media/BBC); *The Vampires of Hollywood, Mark Nelson's Guide to Marriage, Piano Lessons, Occupation, Personal Best* (BBC); *Zombie Rule No.9* (Solus Productions).

LIAM BRENNAN
Duke of Queensberry/Tea Salesman
Royal Lyceum Theatre appearances
The Lieutenant of Inishmore, Of Mice and Men, Mary Queen of Scots Got Her Head Chopped Off, Wondrous Flitting, A View from the Bridge, Romeo and Juliet, Every One, Macbeth, The Winter's Tale, The Merchant of Venice, Anna Karenina and *Othello*.
Recent theatre appearances
Richard III, Twelfth Night (Shakespeare's Globe/The Apollo, West End/Belasco Theatre, Broadway); *Shining City* (Derby Playhouse); *The Deep* (Òran Mór/Edinburgh Festival); *Of Mice and Men* (Perth Theatre); *Tom Fool* (Bush Theatre/Citizens Theatre); *Stranger's Babies, The Found Man, Men in White Suits* (Traverse Theatre); *Tales From Hollywood* (Perth Rep); *Measure for Measure* (Shakespeare's Globe/USA Tour); *Dial M for Murder* (Citizens Theatre); *Edward II, Richard II, Twelfth Night, Macbeth* (Shakespeare's Globe).

IRENE ALLAN
Queen Anne
Royal Lyceum Theatre appearances
Six Characters in Search of an Author, Living Quarters,

The Prime of Miss Jean Brodie, Phaedra, Peter Pan, Macbeth, Sleeping Beauty, The Merchant of Venice

Recent theatre appearances

Lady Windemere's Fan, Present Laughter, Chorus of Disapproval, Hello Dolly (Pitlochry Festival Theatre); *Iron* (Firebrand Theatre Co); *Chelsea Belladonna* (Squarepeg Theatre Co); *Cinderella* (Cumbernauld Theatre Co); *Fergus Lamont, Zlata's Diary* (Communicado); *The Seer* (Dogstar)

Television, film and radio

The Cat, McLevy, Rebus, Heart of Midlothian, For the Love of Willie (BBC Radio 4); *Prostitution* (BBC Scotland).

IFAN MEREDITH

Daniel Defoe/Lord Halifax/Sergeant

Royal Lyceum Theatre appearances

A Midsummer Night's Dream, Living Quarters.

Recent theatre appearances

Peep (Edinburgh Fringe); *The Roman Bath* (Arcola Theatre); *Measure for Measure, Small Change* (Sherman Cymru); *Mincemeat* (Cardboard Citizens); *Romeo and Juliet* (West End); *The English Game* (Headlong); *Frankenstein* (Frantic Assembly); *Hamlet* (The Factory); *A View from the Bridge* (Sheffield Crucible); *Mrs Warren's Profession* (Manchester Royal Exchange); *Much Ado About Nothing* (Bath Theatre Royal); *The Tempest* (The Almeida); *Journey's End* (West End).

Television, film and radio

Dark Matters: Monster Study, Dark Matters: Mesmerise (Discovery Channel); *True Stories: Alexander Graham Bell,*

Holby City, Warriors, Great Expectations (BBC); *Titanic* (ITV/ABC); *Midsomer Murders* (Bentley Productions); *Victoria Cross* (Empire Media); *Murder City* (Granada Television); *The Royal* (Yorkshire Television); *Dr. Jekyll and Mr. Hyde* (Working Title); *Where the Heart Is* (Anglia Television); *Sirens* (S.M.G); *Peak Practice* (Central Television).

ANDREW VINCENT
Duke of Marlborough/Duke of Hamilton
Royal Lyceum Theatre appearances
The Man Who Had All The Luck
Recent theatre appearances
Rougue Herries (Theatre By The Lake Keswick); *Love's Labour's Lost, Merchant of Venice, Antigone, Macbeth* (Northern Broadsides); *Romeo and Juliet, Helen, The Winter's Tale, In Extremis, Under The Black Flag* (Shakespeare's Globe).
Television, film and radio
Secrets and Words, Tracy Beaker Returns, Merlin, Moving On (BBC); *Cold Blood* (ITV); *Magnolia* (Red Productions); *Life on Mars* (Kudos/BBC); *Emmerdale* (Yorkshire Television); *Casanova* (Red Productions).

KEITH FLEMING
Macdonald/Robert Harley/Lord Belhaven
Royal Lyceum Theatre appearances
A Taste of Honey, Trumpets and Raspberries.

Recent theatre appearances

Miss Julie, Scarred for Life (Citizens Theatre); *Macbeth* (Perth Theatre); A *Satire of the Three Estates* (A and BC Theatre Company); *Stones in His Pockets* (Tron Theatre); *The Tempest* (Dundee Rep); *Beautiful Burnout* (Frantic Assembly); *The Making of Us, Black Watch* (National Theatre of Scotland); *Barflies* (Grid Iron); *Doubt* (Theatre Jezebel/Tron Theatre).

Television, film and radio

The Railway Man (The Weinstein Company).

MARK MCDONNELL

Earl of Seafield/William Congreve/Master of House

Royal Lyceum Theatre appearances

Of Mice and Men, Beauty and the Beast, The Importance of Being Earnest, Romeo and Juliet, Curse of the Starving Class, Trumpets and Raspberries, The Merchant of Venice, Six Black Candles, The Breathing House, The Taming of The Shrew, Playboy of the Western World, The Comedy of Errors, Glengarry Glen Ross, The Anatomist.

Recent theatre appearances

The Little Mermaid (Adam Smith, Kirkcaldy); *Death of A Playboy* (Rubber Ear Productions); *Sleeping Beauty, One Million Tiny Plays About Britain* (Citizens Theatre); *Daphnis and Chloe* (Òran Mór); *Honk!* (Royal Derngate Theatre); *Cyprus* (Mull Theatre); *The Little Foxes, Abigail's Party* (Perth Rep).

Television, film and radio

Pantocracy, Nick Nickleby, River City, Victorian Scotland,

Happy Holidays, Ideal, Feel the Force, Still Game, Revolver, Velvet Soup (BBC); *Electric Man, Forward Slash Comedy* (STV); *Rebus, Taggart, Coronation Street* (ITV).
Mark has also appeared in more than 70 plays and readings for BBC Radio 4.

TONY COWNIE
Earl of Stair/Robert Walpole
Royal Lyceum Theatre directing credits
Long Day's Journey Into Night, A Taste of Honey, Mary Queen of Scots Got her Head Chopped Off (co-production with Dundee Rep), Educating Agnes, Romeo and Juliet, The Cherry Orchard, The Beauty Queen of Leenane, Copenhagen, Mary Rose, Trumpets and Raspberries, Vanity Fair, Mrs Warren's Profession, Tartuffe, Laurel and Hardy, A Life in the Theatre, The Taming of the Shrew, The Playboy of the Western World, Sleeping Beauty, The Princess and the Goblin, Miseryguts, Beauty and the Beast, The Comedy of Errors, Britannia Rules, Three Sisters, The Hypochondriak and Cinderella.
Other directing credits include *Backpacker Blues (Òran Mór); The Woman Who Cooked Her Husband (Tour); The Laird O' Grippy (Dundee Rep); the Herald Angel-winning Empty Jesters (Traverse); Shanghaied (Nippy Sweeties); The King of Scotland (Talking Dogs);Tartuffe (QMC); Aladdin, Cinderella and Sleeping Beauty (King's Theatre, Glasgow); Two (Tour); the acclaimed and highly successful Tutti Frutti (National Theatre of Scotland) and the UK Holocaust Memorial ceremony at the Usher Hall.*

Tony has worked extensively as an actor in Scottish theatre with companies including The Lyceum, TAG, Communicado, Nippy Sweeties, Citizens, Tron, Traverse and Dundee Rep Theatre. He has also worked with Nottingham Playhouse and the Gate Theatre, London. He won The Stage 'Best Actor' Award 1999 for *A Madman Sings to the Moon* (Brunton) and was nominated for TMA 'Best Actor' Award for the same role at The Lyceum in 2004.

REBECCA PALMER
Sarah Churchill/Favour
Television, film and radio
MI High, Nearly Famous (Kudos); *Mary's Ride* (Okofilm Productions); *Flytopia* (Karni & Saul/Film4); *Garrow's Law* (Shed Media); *Fiona's Story* (BBC Scotland); *New Town Killers* (NTK Films/Richard Jobson); *Blood Trails* (K5 Films); *This Filthy Earth* (Tall Stories/Film4); *Intimacy* (Green Point Productions).

CREATIVE BIOGRAPHIES

MARK THOMSON
Director

Mark has been Artistic Director of The Royal Lyceum
Theatre Company since April 2003, during which time he
has directed *Dark Road, Takin' Over The Asylum,
Cinderella, The Marriage of Figaro, The Lieutenant of
Inishmore*, Shakespeare's *The Winter's Tale, Julius Caesar,
Othello, As You Like It* and *The Merchant of Venice*; Oscar
Wilde's *The Importance of Being Earnest*; Pirandello's *Six
Characters in Search of an Author* (co-production with the
National Theatre of Scotland and Citizens Theatre);
premières of Jo Clifford's *Every One* and Goethe's *Faust*
parts one and two; *Six Black Candles* and *Monks* by Des
Dillon; John Byrne's *Uncle Varick*; his own plays: *A
Madman Sings to the Moon* and *Pinocchio*; his adaptation of
James Hogg's *Private Memoirs* and *Confessions of a
Justified Sinner* and, in 2011, the acclaimed *Wondrous
Flitting*.

Mark was Artistic Director of the Brunton Theatre
Company from 1997 to 2002, directing 21 shows and
winning a Herald Angel Award for his play *A Madman
Sings to the Moon*, and a Scotsman Fringe First and a
Herald Angel Award for his play *Moving Objects*. Prior to
that, he was Assistant Director at the Theatre Royal
Stratford East and the Royal Shakespeare Company and
Associate Director at Nottingham Playhouse.

TIM BARROW
Writer

Tim's debut stage play *Guy* was produced at London's Pleasance Theatre. *Union* is his second play.

Tim wrote, produced and starred in *The Inheritance* (Lyre Productions, Raindance Award British Independent Film Awards, Nominated for Best Producer BAFTA Scotland New Talent Awards 2008); he also wrote, produced and directed the film *The Space Between* and was the assistant director and co-producer of the world premiere of *Blue On Blue* (Shotgun/Theatre 503) directed by Tom Hardy.

Tim trained as an actor at Drama Centre London. His theatre credits include Stoirm Og's Scottish tour of *The Idiot At The Wall*, plus productions for Citizens Theatre, The Arches, Theatre 503, Bard In The Botanics, Prime Productions, Theatre Enigma and Nonsenseroom. Screen acting appearances include *Taggart*, *Waterloo Road*, *Children Of The Dead End* (Glass Machine); *The Queen's Wedding* (Mentorn); Richard Jobson's *New Town Killers*; *The Tony Miller Story* (BBC Alba) and *Narcopolis* (T Squared Films).

ANDRZEJ GOULDING
Designer and Video Artist

Andrzej studied Stage Design at Central Saint Martins and his previous work on The Lyceum stage includes *The Last Witch* (Edinburgh International Festival).

Video design credits
Sane New World (Ruby Wax Tour); *From Morning To Midnight* (National Theatre); *Coriolanus* (Donmar Warehouse); *The Machine* (Manchester International Festival, NY Armoury); *Groove on Down The Road* (Southbank Centre); *Relative Values* (Theatre Royal Bath); *Hannah* (Unicorn Theatre); *The Girl of the Golden West, Carousel* (Opera North); *Othello, Twelfth Night* (Singapore Rep Theatre); *DNA* (Hull Truck/Tour); *Silent Night* (Philadelphia Opera); *Amadeus* (Maltz Jupiter Theatre, Florida); *Mass Observation* (Almeida Theatre); *Maria* (Wexford Opera Festival).

Animation credits
Ghost The Musical (Colin Ingram Ltd); *Love Never Dies, Wizard of Oz* (Really Useful Group).

Assistant/Associate set design credits
The Lord of the Rings (the musical)(Kevin Wallace Ltd); *Ghost The Musical* (Colin Ingram Ltd.); *Matilda The Musical* (Royal Shakespeare Company); *Boeing Boeing* (Sonia Friedman).

CHRIS DAVEY
Lighting Designer

Chris has designed extensively for National Theatre, Royal Shakespeare Company, Royal Court, Royal Exchange Manchester, West Yorkshire Playhouse, Birmingham Rep and Hampstead Theatre. He has won three CATS Best Design Awards for *Anna Karenina* at Royal Lyceum, Edinburgh and *Beauty and the Beast* and *Peer Gynt* at Dundee Rep Theatre. He also won the TMA Best Lighting Design for *Dial M for Murder* (West Yorkshire Playhouse) and *Beyond the Horizon* (Royal and Derngate, Northampton).

Royal Lyceum Theatre credits
Takin' Over the Asylum (co-production with Citizens Theatre); *Beauty and The Beast, The Lieutenant of Inishmore, Peter Pan, Vanity Fair, The Glass Menagerie, Six Characters in Search of an Author, The Merchant of Venice, Art, Anna Karenina, The Prime of Miss Jean Brodie, The Playboy of the Western World, Lavender Blue, The Deep Blue Sea, Clay Bull*
Other theatre design credits
Sweeney Todd (West Yorkshire Playhouse/Royal Exchange); Betrayal (Citizens Theatre); *Anna Karenina, The Firebird, Sweeney Todd, Who's Afraid of Virginia Woolf, Romeo and Juliet, Peer Gynt* (Dundee Rep); *The Last Witch, Three Thousand Troubled Threads* (Edinburgh International Festival); *The Three Musketeers, Pornography, Family, Passing Places, Greta* (Traverse); *When I Was a Girl I Used*

to Scream and Shout, Twelfth Night, Moving Objects
(Brunton); *One Flew Over the Cuckoo's Nest, Levelland*
(Assembly Rooms); *The Vagina Monologues* (Playhouse);
Matthew Bourne's *The Car Man* (Festival Theatre) and
The Lord of the Flies (Theatre Royal, Glasgow).

MEGAN BAKER
Costume Designer

Megan has been designing costumes professionally for 25
years. She also runs the BA Hons and Masters Performance
Costume courses at Edinburgh College of Art, University of
Edinburgh and has supervised the costumes for over 50
productions including shows for the West End and The
Globe Theatre.

Royal Lyceum Theatre credits
The Guid Sisters (co-production with the National Theatre
of Scotland).
Costume design credits
ANA (Imago, Montreal/Stellar Quines, Scotland); *Village
on the Roof* (Kickabout films); *A Midsummer Night's Dream*
(Brunton Theatre); *The Invisible Man* (Vaudeville Theatre,
West End); *The Curse of the Werewolf, Dog eat Dog, Rent
Money, Funny Black Women on the Edge, Gulp Fiction, Do
Yer Eat With Yer Fingers, Back to Basics, Goin' Local*
(Theatre Royal Stratford East); *The Waterfall* (Riverside
Studios); *The Ten Commandments* (Place Theatre);

The Challenge (Shaw Theatre); *The Duchess of Malfi* (Point Blank).

PHILIP PINSKY
Composer and Sound Designer

Royal Lyceum Theatre credits
Dark Road, Time and the Conways, The Guid Sisters, Mary Queen of Scots Got Her Head Chopped Off, Wondrous Flitting, Educating Agnes, Age of Arousal, The Importance of Being Earnest, Romeo and Juliet, Every One, Peter Pan, Confessions of a Justified Sinner, Copenhagen, The Lion the Witch and The Wardrobe, Mary Rose, Macbeth, Trumpets and Raspberries, The Glass Menagerie, Living Quarters, The Winter's Tale, The Merchant of Venice, Faust 1 & 2.
Other theatre credits
Leaving Planet Earth (EIF/Grid Iron); *The List* (Stellar Quines); *Kora* (Magnetic North/Dundee Rep); *Chaos and Contingency, Humanimalia* (Janis Claxton Dance); *Christine, La Reine Garcon* (Theatre du Noveau Monde, Montreal); *ANA* (Imago, Montreal/Stellar Quines, Scotland); *Spring Awakening, Decky Does a Bronco 2010* (Grid Iron/Traverse); *After the End* (Edinburgh Fringe/Dundee Rep); *Huxley's Lab* (Grid Iron/Lung Ha's).
Recent television credits
Art and Soul, Ninewells, Harley Street, Seaside Rescue, What Not to Wear (BBC); The Art of Faith, Anthony Gormley & the 4th Plinth (Sky Arts).

Phillip has also worked on education projects for Scottish Chamber Orchestra and the National Theatre of Scotland. He was winner of the Critics Award for Theatre in Scotland 2005 for best use of music in theatre and of a Sony Music Award for Extraneous Noise Off (BBC Radio 3).

BECKY PALMER
Assistant Director

Recent director credits
The Hen Night (Royal Conservatoire of Scotland/Cockpit/Traverse); *Like a Moth to a Flame* (The Arches/Royal Conservatoire of Scotland); *The Winter's Tale* (Shakespeare's Globe/Royal Conservatoire of Scotland); *Riot Squat* (Thrive Theatre/Fringe Festival).
Recent assistant director credits
Women Beware Women (Royal Conservatoire of Scotland); *A Clockwork Orange* (Action to The Word).

Becky is currently Assistant Director of the upcoming production *Tomorrow* (Vanishing Point).
She is a recent graduate of the Royal Conservatoire of Scotland and Artistic Director of Thrive Theatre Co.

All scenery, costumes and props made in the Royal Lyceum Theatre Edinburgh workshops at Roseburn.

For my parents

The Royal Lyceum Theatre Company

'As one of Scotland's largest producing companies, The Lyceum enriches lives and our culture.' Brian Cox CBE, Honorary Patron

The Royal Lyceum Theatre Company is one of Scotland's leading producing drama companies, with an excellent reputation for both classical and contemporary work. Our aim is to introduce as wide an audience as possible to the colourful and imaginative world of drama.

Committed to developing and supporting creative talent, we commission new work, stage contemporary plays and re-imagine classic theatre, as well as work alongside a selection of both prominent and progressive theatre companies from across the UK.

With our strong Creative Learning programme, we deliver projects and training to schools, companies and individuals. Our Lyceum Youth Theatre, one of Scotland's biggest and best-established youth theatre companies, involves over 300 young people ranging from 5 to 18 years old.

All of this takes place within our beautiful late Victorian building in the West End of Edinburgh. Costumes and sets for Lyceum productions are created and built by our team in our workshops at Roseburn, while the Company rehearse in the building opposite the theatre. This all comes together to create high quality theatre in a wonderful setting.

For more information about us, please visit lyceum.org.uk, like us on Facebook, or follow @lyceumtheatre on Twitter.

The Royal Lyceum Theatre Company
30b Grindlay Street
Edinburgh
EH3 9AX
0131 248 4848 | lyceum.org.uk

Registered Company No. SC062065 and Registered Charity No. SC010509

The Scots

Allan Ramsay
MacDonald
Grace
Favour
Earl of Seafield
Earl of Stair
Duke of Queensberry
Duke of Hamilton
Lord Belhaven
Sergeant Campbell

The English

Daniel Defoe
Queen Anne
Sarah Churchill, Duchess of Marlborough
Daffyd Wyn Davies
William, Master of Queen Anne's Household
John Churchill, Duke of Marlborough
Lord Halifax
Robert Walpole
William Congreve
Robert Harley

ACT I

Scene 1   The Saltyre

A dreich, wet, windy, cold Edinburgh night. Interior of a dark, smoky, drink-sodden watering hole in the poorer part of town named "The Saltyre." Locals hide in the shadows. Alcoholics people the bar. God it's ugly.

Door opens with a bang.

ALLAN RAMSAY, an energetic young man supports / drags a STRANGER in –

RAMSAY
Macdonald! Macdonald!

RAMSAY plonks him into a chair.

Owner appears – MACDONALD – a man who's seen it all & been left unimpressed.

RAMSAY
Quickly, man!

MACDONALD
You're drenched.

RAMSAY
Whisky!
Found him in the close, half dead.
He's been fleeced and dumped.

MACDONALD
Fine threads. Obviously got a bit of cash.

RAMSAY
No longer.

MACDONALD
What d'you think? Soldier?

RAMSAY
Check the boots – French leather.
Get him some whisky and we'll discover his secrets.

MACDONALD heads off.

RAMSAY
Ye poor bastard.
Some wee urchins nailed you.
Can you hear us? Hey?

RAMSAY slaps his face. STRANGER jerks into consciousness – instantly feels pain. Blinks at RAMSAY.

RAMSAY

Yer no dead yet.

Ah'd make a poor ferryman.

You've been mugged, sonny.

MACDONALD appears with a bottle of whisky and glass. RAMSAY takes the glass, pours a measure... downs it himself. Pours another, opens the STRANGER'S mouth, chucks the drink in. STRANGER swallows, chokes, coughs, comes to...

RAMSAY

Welcome tae Edinburgh!

Beer's rough, and the locals reckless.

We ken what you are.

An outlaw.

Renegade on the run. Housewife's secret rapture.

And ah ken what you need.

Poetry.

Ah'll make you a legend.

Ha'penny per ode. Do you a pamphlet.

Mysterious debaucher, sinister /debonair. Trace of cavalier.

Lassies'll be gagging for you.

Start wi a dozen?

Half?

2?

STRANGER just stares at him.

RAMSAY

Allan Ramsay. Wig-maker.

Writer too – seriously! Poems, stories.

Gonnae start a theatre – adore actresses.

Ma auditorium right here.

We're born storytellers.

The mercat cross – thronging for news – Grassmarket for the hangings.

Been a shocking year.

Failed harvests. Bread extortionate. Everything goes up.

Drink. Disease. Taxes.

Riots in Glasgow. Nothing new there.

Yer first visit?

STRANGER nods.

RAMSAY

S'a hell of pretty town if you hold yer nose.

Oh, ah'll show you the sights!

The Royal Mile, that's the road you got mugged in –

St Giles, our Kirk –

STRANGER

Kirk?

RAMSAY

No Cathedral – bit of a dust-up with Rome.

The Palace, the castle, sewage flooding the streets.

All part of the Embra charm!

Door opens. An elegantly-dressed man enters cautiously. John Dalrymple, the EARL OF STAIR. Skulks over to a corner table, hides in shadows.

RAMSAY

And the scummiest nobility in Christendom.

The Earl of Stair. A wolf in wolf's clothing.

Politician with a penchant for massacres and wee-bit foreign royalty.

Advocates the Highlands without a single Highlander.

Coat of arms display 9 diamonds – the Curse of Scotland.

His brother's President of the Court of Session.

Justice remains bound and gagged in their darkest cellar.

Door opens again. In comes another well-dressed man. James Ogilvie, the EARL OF SEAFIELD. He's nervous. Surveys his surroundings.

RAMSAY

And our Lord Chancellor, the Earl of Seafield.

He rules Parliament.

Rumours say he has an army of bastards, secretly rotting in prisons.

Betrays the poor. Fills his own pockets instead.

The corruption drives a man tae drink. Oi, Macdonald!

MACDONALD comes over.

RAMSAY

The Saltyre's owner – supplier of the finest whores in town.
Beer's seductive n' all.

RAMSAY spins him a coin.

MACDONALD

Grave robbing again, Ramsay?

RAMSAY

Just plying ma trade.

MACDONALD

There's been a spate of baldness?

RAMSAY

Been drinking your ale.
Our invalid needs to be revived.

MACDONALD

Looks alright to me.

RAMSAY

On Death's threshold, Macdonald! Without sustenance,
he'll perish!

MACDONALD gets him a drink.

RAMSAY

Ah'm from a wee place in Lanarkshire – Leadhills?

Nah, no-one's ever heard of it.
Ah'm putting it on the map.
...
Talkative aren't you?
What are you?

STRANGER
Writer.

RAMSAY
Company of equals!!
What d'you write – poems? Stories?

STRANGER
Some.

RAMSAY
Yer English.

Beat.

RAMSAY
So's ma mother – s'no a crime. Folk here dinnae care –
Unless yer Catholic – then there'll be lynchings.
Where you from?

STRANGER
London.

RAMSAY
What's that like?

STRANGER
Wretched.

RAMSAY
You'll fit right in!
What brings you north?
Latest novel?
A bloodthirsty revenge thriller??

STRANGER
An ancient doomed love affair.

RAMSAY
Aye??

*Door bangs open and GRACE arrives. She's a prostitute and
has had a hard day.*

RAMSAY
The Saltyre's rose among thorns.

GRACE
Fuck I'm fucked.
Lust-lovin' Lord Elphinstone.
Arse hangs like a soggy curtain.
He sang me a lullaby then rode me til I bled.
Drink.

She chucks a coin at MACDONALD.

GRACE
Still scribbling, Ramsay?
Who's the new tart?

RAMSAY
Ah don't write for tarts, ah write cos –

GRACE
Yer horny!

RAMSAY
Cos ah'm moved –

GRACE
By yer groin.

RAMSAY
By my soul!

GRACE
Och, ah'll move you Allan.

She cuddles into him.

GRACE
Hear you've money.
Fancy a flutter?

RAMSAY
Marry me, Grace?

GRACE
When yer scribbling can pay ma rent.

RAMSAY
Ah'll give you fame.

GRACE
Yer a boy.

RAMSAY
"O Katy will you gang wi' me,
And leave the dinsome town a while,
The blossom's sprouting frae the tree
And a' the summer's gawn to smile;
The mavis, nightingale and lark,
The bleating lambs and whistling hind,
In ilka dale, green, shaw and park,
Will nourish health, and glad yer mind."

Beat.

GRACE
Yer no getting a shag.

RAMSAY
That's ma fortune. Right there.

GRACE
Dreams.

RAMSAY
Ah'll make em fly.

GRACE
You talk such shite.
Who's yer beat-up pal?

RAMSAY
A tourist. Got jumped in the close.

MACDONALD deposits 2 drinks beside them.

RAMSAY
Hope you took them rats out.
S'no the pox that makes folk blind, it's your beer.

MACDONALD
If you're going blind Ramsay, best give up the hand jobs.

MACDONALD stomps off as GRACE picks up his book.

GRACE
Always with books.
What's this one?

RAMSAY
Catullus.

GRACE

The fuck's he?

RAMSAY

"No woman can say she's been loved so much,
As my lover in truth's adored by me.
No faith in any love's bond was such,
As that found, on my part, in love of thee."
...
Roman poet.
In love with a courtesan.
She was high class but betrayed him.

GRACE

Hookers have no class.
Speaking of which...

*She has seen the EARL OF STAIR, a valued customer, and
makes her move.*

But MACDONALD gets there first –

MACDONALD

Can we assist?
Forgive me, Lord Chancellor??

STAIR

Give us privacy.

And bring some oysters.

Better be decent.

Or I'll have you skewered over your own fire.

MACDONALD bows, moves off.

SEAFIELD

Here, Stair? You suggest this midden?

STAIR

Needs must when the devil drives.

SEAFIELD

We'll be lynched!

STAIR

Keep yer voice down!

Anonymity will be preserved if you behave yerself.

GRACE makes her move.

GRACE

Look what the cat dragged in!

Johnny "sweet-cheeks" Dalrymple. What joy!

SEAFIELD

Christ, Stair!

STAIR

We're old friends.

SEAFIELD

Is she safe?

STAIR

From all but the pox.

GRACE

Unfair, Jonny. Ma body's pure as a politician.
Gonna introduce us to yer friend?

STAIR

Lord Seafield, meet the least undesirable prostitute
Edinburgh may offer.

SEAFIELD

Charmed, my lady.

GRACE

For your coin I can be.

STAIR

Not now, Grace, we're otherwise engaged.

GRACE

Well you know where to find me.

She moves off.

Respectfully, MACDONALD serves a dish of oysters.

SEAFIELD
You own this place?

MACDONALD
Sir.

SEAFIELD
In Her Majesty's name, we charge you to observe our privacy.

SEAFIELD tastes an oyster.

SEAFIELD
Curious aroma. Familiar, can't quite place it.
Name?

MACDONALD
Macdonald, sir.

SEAFIELD
Then you'll be acquainted with the Earl of Stair.
Family? In Glencoe?

MACDONALD
My sister.

SEAFIELD
Oh, bad luck.

MACDONALD leaves.

STAIR
Discretion, Seafield.

SEAFIELD
Hmm?

STAIR
Leave the damned Highlanders be.

SEAFIELD
Macdonald death-rattles pricking yer conscience?

STAIR
To business.

SEAFIELD
Will you not wine and dine me first?

STAIR
I'm not here to fuck you.

Beat.

SEAFIELD
The succession vexes.
Queen Anne is childless. 17 pregnancies without success.

Danish semen struggles in this climate.

The former Royal family lives exiled in France.

Their Jacobite "Pretender" itches to step nobly into the breach.

STAIR

Catholic.

SEAFIELD

Scottish. Stuart. Like Anne.

How much longer will Westminster bear the barren queen?

STAIR

They'll never stomach a Catholic dynasty!

SEAFIELD

Will they digest a Hanoverian one?!

Do you like sauerkraut? Fucking vile.

STAIR

The upcoming Union act.

Rumours abound we haven't enough votes.

Hamilton's rhetoric gains more disciples.

SEAFIELD

Destiny will not be rushed, Stair –

STAIR

Damned Commissioners need to get their fingers out –

SEAFIELD

Providence rewards.

We possess an ace in the pack.

STAIR

Queensberry?!

SEAFIELD

The fat Duke scents his prize.

English land. Girls. Boys. Audience for his imperious rhetoric.

A new era looms before us.

STAIR

And once Scotland's sold to the highest bidder?

SEAFIELD

The only bidder.

Initially, we turned the English down.

Fortunately, they improved the bid substantially.

SEAFIELD kicks back with an oyster.

SEAFIELD

We're practically there.

One monarch.

The Union of the Crowns.

Charles II was gagging for full union, but got sidetracked by actresses.

STAIR

Thank God for his brother.

Tyrants get things done.

There'll be riots.

Once people sniff marriage with Westminster –

SEAFIELD

People have but one loyalty.

Bread is their parliament, be it Edinburgh or London.

Observe our nation!

Like Charles's mistresses, we're on our knees.

Even God's abandoned Scotland.

The poor don't want romance, they want food for their bairns.

This country needs leaders.

And, as patriots, Stair, we shall lead them.

They tuck into oysters with relish. THE STRANGER appears at their table.

STRANGER

Gentlemen.

STAIR

What are you?

STRANGER

Humble servant, sir, bringing a message.

STAIR
From whom?

STRANGER
Fellow patriots across the border.

STAIR
We do not know you, sir.

SEAFIELD
Keep yer grubby paws away.

STRANGER displays a piece of paper.

STRANGER
Westminster's love letter.
The full list.
Men of honour and their rewards.
Your name is eighth, Lord Stair.
And the bribe.

SEAFIELD
Preposterous!
There's no list –

STRANGER
That's you at the top, Lord Seafield.

SEAFIELD reads.

STRANGER

My name is Daniel Defoe and I carry Her Majesty's authority.

A crucial act comes before your Parliament.

Only when passed will each lord receive his pay.

STAIR

Ours is a democratic parliament, Mr Defoe.

Votes cannot be predicted nor bought.

DEFOE

His Grace, the Duke of Atholl - £1,000 –

His Grace, the Earl of Marchmont - £1,104 –

STAIR

Yes –

DEFOE

Merely £490, Lord Seafield?

SEAFIELD

Alright!!

DEFOE

Her Majesty wishes you guide each man's conscience

To vote as he has sworn.

SEAFIELD

And if not?

DEFOE

Queen Anne does not confide in me...
But country-wide circulation of this list,
And full-scale English invasion, I should think.

STAIR

Too cocky, Defoe.
We butcher English spies.
The City Watch will decapitate you before sunset.

SEAFIELD

String you up by your insolent eyeballs first!

DEFOE

I'm protected.

STAIR

By your lunatic Queen?

DEFOE

Robert Harley has taken me under his wing.

STAIR

You're a long way from London, son.

DEFOE

I back myself in city slums against you, my Lord.
No Campbell militia here.
The Curse of Scotland?!
How many hidden knives are eager for your blood?

Let's start with the landlord.

...

In town a few days, sampling the hospitality. Beer could be
better.

I need, my lords, signatures from each patriot to take south.

Every love note deserves a reply.

STAIR

If it should prove not possible?

DEFOE

Farewell titles and privilege.

Not to mention the wrath of an Edinburgh mob,

When they discover what their country was sold for.

SEAFIELD

How may we contact you?

DEFOE

I'll make a point of looking you up before I go.

Been delightful chatting, my Lords.

Enjoy those oysters.

He leaves.

STAIR

£490?

SEAFIELD

We are not greedy, Stair.
Is he genuine?

STAIR

How else did he get that list?
If he's Harley's pet, we must tread cautiously.
We need to see Queensberry.

They leave. RAMSAY & MACDONALD watch them.

RAMSAY

Your establishment's going up in the world.
Think they noticed?

MACDONALD

Notice what?

RAMSAY

Their shellfish's been swimming in urine?
Nobility. They'll put anything in their mouths.

Scene 2   **The English Court**

Palace of Kensington, London.

Doors swing open to reveal the magnificent reception chamber at the court of QUEEN ANNE. Fountains gush, columns rear skywards, doves flutter. QUEEN ANNE, a short, dreamy, lazily-dressed woman, is choosing tea. Attending Her Majesty is SARAH, DUCHESS OF MARLBOROUGH, the love of her life.

Attending them, with his wares, is an enthusiastic TEA SALESMAN.

SALESMAN
Chinese Your Majesty.

QUEEN ANNE reaches her hand into the leaves. Stirs them around.

SALESMAN
Compliments of the Emperor Kangxi.
A man of impeccable taste.

QUEEN ANNE is unimpressed. The SALESMAN shimmers to the next case.

SALESMAN
Possibly this one? The Ambassador's personal favourite. Assam.

SARAH

We liked him, darling. He had a stammer and a glass eye.

QUEEN ANNE holds out her hand. The SALESMAN moves forward and proffers a prepared cup of Assam. QUEEN ANNE takes the smallest mouthful. Considers.

QUEEN ANNE

Charcoal.

Nonplussed, the SALESMAN moves to the next.

SALESMAN

Another popular choice. From Ceylon.

SARAH

Oh the last lot was super divine!
We filled a whole bath with it at Blenheim!

SALESMAN

The most delicate flavours.

QUEEN ANNE tests them again.

QUEEN ANNE

Smells like...

SALESMAN

Bergamot?

QUEEN ANNE
... Cat piss.

SARAH
Next!

They move to the next. SALESMAN is getting slightly desperate.

SALESMAN
Then perhaps my personal preference?
From the Indian subcontinent, shipped from Darjeeling...

QUEEN ANNE
Revolting. Truly revolting.

SARAH
Any more?

SALESMAN is flustered.

SALESMAN
Well, I had hoped...

QUEEN ANNE
What's this?

She's moved to the final box – smaller, less grand –

SALESMAN
It's not really —

QUEEN ANNE
There's fruit in here.

SALESMAN
Lord Grey brought it —

QUEEN ANNE
Lemons?

SARAH
Lemons??

SALESMAN
We know little about it —

SARAH
Is this a joke?

SALESMAN
He says it improves —

SARAH
Do you mock your sovereign?

SALESMAN
No, Ma'am!

SARAH
The last tea broker. Go on. Ask what happened.

SALESMAN
... What??

QUEEN ANNE
He tried overpricing.

SARAH
And was packed off to the Tower!

SALESMAN
The *Tower??*

QUEEN ANNE
Being sovereign is like tea.

SALESMAN
... Bursting with flavour?!

QUEEN ANNE
Works best with sweetening.
Let's swap. For a day.

She hands him the crown from her head.

QUEEN ANNE
Put it on. I command you.

SALESMAN cautiously puts on the crown.

QUEEN ANNE
Now dance around.

SALESMAN
Dance?

SARAH
You heard her. Dance.

SALESMAN
... Hornpipe? Gavotte?

QUEEN ANNE
Dance as if picking tea leaves on the sun-kissed slopes of a mountain.

SALESMAN
... Sun-kissed?

QUEEN ANNE
Morning dew fresh on the buds, snow-drenched Himalayas beyond.

SALESMAN cautiously begins to dance –

QUEEN ANNE
No, no, the Himalayas!

SALESMAN incorporates the Himalayas into his dance.

QUEEN ANNE
Your legs are too stiff. Here –

She begins to dance also, showing him the way.

*JOHN CHURCHILL, DUKE OF MARLBOROUGH
makes his entrance. A military monster – bluff, bad-tempered,
brutal. The MASTER attends him. QUEEN ANNE stops
dancing. SALESMAN, not knowing whether to stop or not,
doesn't...*

SARAH
Johnnie! We're trying tea.

MARLBOROUGH
What kinda palace d'you run, Annie?!
Thieves everywhere!
Slippery bastard tried stealing me hat!

SARAH
Just being attentive, dear –

MARLBOROUGH
Tried to nick it! Off my own fucking head!
Mugged as soon as I fucking *entered!*

QUEEN ANNE
I'll have him dismissed.

MARLBOROUGH

Flay him alive! When soldiers transgress –

MARLBOROUGH sees the SALESMAN dancing with the crown of England –

MARLBOROUGH

WHAT THE DEVIL ARE YOU DOING, SIR?!

SALESMAN

... My lord?

MARLBOROUGH belts him –

MARLBOROUGH

YOUR GRACE! I'M A FUCKING DUKE!!

SALESMAN

Your Grace, sorry, your Grace –

MARLBOROUGH

The crown sir, the crown!

SALESMAN whips it off his head.

MARLBOROUGH

Most sacred circlet on this isle!
And you dare, you DARE adorn yer brow with it??

SALESMAN
But she –

MARLBOROUGH
Name!

SALESMAN
Davies sir. Daffyd Wyn Davies.

MARLBOROUGH
Irish??

SALESMAN
... From the Rhondda –

MARLBOROUGH
What you playing at, employing the paddies?!
Papist assassins!

SARAH
Darling, he's not –

MARLBOROUGH
Bog-loving potato-faeries!
Give em an inch, they plough up an acreage.
I'll have ya flogged sir! FLOGGED!
GET OUT!!

SALESMAN
Right-oh.

MARLBOROUGH
CROWN!

SALESMAN returns the crown to QUEEN ANNE. He leaves, but can't quite resist...

SALESMAN
If you change your mind, we have an offer on Assam –

MARLBOROUGH
OUT!!

SALESMAN leaves swiftly.

MARLBOROUGH
Should've wiped em out like Cromwell!

QUEEN ANNE
They come in handy – wars, suchlike...

SARAH
Fancy a brew? Every kind you could wish for.

MARLBOROUGH
No time, Sarah! Bring news!

QUEEN ANNE
Oh?

MARLBOROUGH

Parliament. New Bill.

They plan to increase your island.

QUEEN ANNE

Can one increase an island?

MARLBOROUGH

You get the northern bit.

QUEEN ANNE

... Cumberland?

MARLBOROUGH

Scotland. Where the Scots live.

QUEEN ANNE

Thought I had it. Got their crown somewhere.

MARLBOROUGH

We unify the land. Single Parliament.

Not even paying *that* much...

QUEEN ANNE

Can one buy a country? Willie, is this true?

MASTER

They are calling it The Act of Union, Ma'am.

MARLBOROUGH
We shall become... Great Britain.

A stunned silence.

QUEEN ANNE
Why?

MARLBOROUGH
MEN HAVE DIED DAMMIT!
Legions of Englishmen defending your realm!
Decades I've preserved this island!
Surrounded by bastards who hate us!

QUEEN ANNE
The Jews?

MARLBOROUGH
France!
Rumours, Annie! Alliance with the Scots!
Revolution! Insurrection –

QUEEN ANNE
When will this happen?

MASTER
The Bill is being proposed on Friday, Ma'am.

QUEEN ANNE
And when shall it come into force?

MASTER
Lunchtime.

QUEEN ANNE
Well...
Has the hour reached eleven?

MASTER
Indeed it has, Ma'am.

QUEEN ANNE
Splendid! Time for tea.
Let's try some of Lord Grey's lemony stuff.

The MASTER bows and leaves. Tea is poured.

QUEEN ANNE
The Scots.

SARAH
The Scots.

QUEEN ANNE
The Scots.
Constant thorn in our flesh.
Buggers forced me to sign that Act of Security.
But you need Scots for your armies...

MARLBOROUGH
Damned good fighters. Beasts!

SARAH

Europe grows restless, rulers ambitious.

Jacobism rears its head, encouraged by France.

Louis would place your step-brother on the throne.

QUEEN ANNE

What if young James landed here with an army?

Would the country support me over the dashing Jacobite Prince?

SARAH

The people love you, Majesty.

QUEEN ANNE

An aging woman, no direct successor...

SARAH

Harley's diplomacy?

QUEEN ANNE

I want security, not toothless treaties.

Europe rips herself asunder despite gallons of diplomatic ink.

MARLBOROUGH

Nothing so persuasive as a cavalry charge.

SARAH

This century stirs from slumber, darling,
And we cannot be caught sleeping.
Already there's unrest in the counties.

QUEEN ANNE

Satirists mock my stillborns.

SARAH

Then this treaty shall trump their scorn.
A legacy to outlast your luckless family's.

QUEEN ANNE

Unity. Durability. Tea.
Fitting testament to our reign.
Marlborough.
Bring me the Act of Union.

MARLBOROUGH, sensing the occasion, bows.

The MASTER arrives with tray of tea things. Plus...

QUEEN ANNE

Buns!
Oh Willie, you are good!

MASTER

I live but to serve.

MARLBOROUGH

Your Majesty, every sinew shall be strained.
Parliament shall pass this Bill.

QUEEN ANNE

Excellent.

MARLBOROUGH

And if any bastard tries to abstain...!

SARAH

Run him thru, darling, that's the spirit.
And get Harley onto it. He's incredibly good.
Please now excuse us.

MARLBOROUGH bows solemnly and exits. The ladies sit.

QUEEN ANNE

Is he ever calm?

SARAH

Only in battle. He rages in his sleep.

QUEEN ANNE

Suppose I should be thankful.
Hate to face him across a rugged moorland.
Will it work, darling?
Already the Welsh and Irish hate me.

SARAH

Can't George just try a little harder?

QUEEN ANNE

We've tried fucking.

All it brings are stillborns and weaklings.

SARAH

George's sperm, darling. Milk-water.

QUEEN ANNE

I've decreased the laudanum.

Brings on migraines.

What would you do?

SARAH

Fight on.

Johnnie will manage the treaty.

And Harley, well, he always works.

We shall keep you safe.

Now, let's forget these trivialities and have a gorgeous afternoon.

Tea is poured. SARAH motions – the MASTER signals music to begin.

Scene 3　　　　　**The Saltyre**

Edinburgh.

Raining hard again. Tavern filled by folk sheltering from the weather. RAMSAY splaffs with MACDONALD.

RAMSAY
Take light. What is it?

MACDONALD
Eh?

RAMSAY
Candlelight catches our eye, illuminates.
How?

MACDONALD
... You just light the wick –

RAMSAY
Aye, you spark the tinder, there's flames.
What's in those flames?

MACDONALD
A whore's smile.

RAMSAY
Channel the light – shine it through glass.
What d'you see? Colour!

MACDONALD
Buy another drink, Ramsay...

RAMSAY hands him a glass –

RAMSAY
Hold it.

RAMSAY positions a candle underneath.

RAMSAY
Hold it steady and tilt.
Look at the sides – what d'you see?

MACDONALD
An empty pint, Ramsay.

RAMSAY
What's the candlelight doing?

MACDONALD
Shining. It...
Wait... There!

RAMSAY
Hold it steady.

MACDONALD
Purple! Purple shadows...
Yellow?

RAMSAY
Down the bottom. Red?

MACDONALD
Aye! Fuck me!

MACDONALD drops the glass –

MACDONALD
Do it again!

RAMSAY
Need another glass. A full one!

GRACE enters.

RAMSAY
The Huntress returns. Welcome Diana.
Talk light with me Grace.
What's it made from?

GRACE
The ground-down bones of pox-ridden whores,
Cut down in the prime of their forsaken lives.

RAMSAY
Brittle white bones.

GRACE
Fragile as promises.

RAMSAY
Fancy a flutter?

GRACE
Nae cash.

RAMSAY
Gamble with mine.

GRACE
Made of money now?

RAMSAY
Sold a pamphlet.
Bishop Rose wanted some anonymous anti-English prose.
Plus some dirty limericks on the side.
C'mon, we'll split it half 'n half.

GRACE
Don't you waste enough money on me?

RAMSAY
'Tis a particular honour, m'lady!

GRACE
Ah'll buy you parchment when ah win.
You can be filthy as long as yer ink holds out.

They play cards.

RAMSAY
Wrote new poems.

GRACE
More Ides?

RAMSAY
Odes!
Nah. Sonnets.

GRACE
Sonnets?

RAMSAY
A form of lyric poetry comprising 14 lines,
Observing a strict rhyming structure.

GRACE
Ah've heard sonnets, Ramsay.
This guy used to quote them.
Fastest way tae get me on ma back.

RAMSAY
Who?

GRACE
Some laddie who had witchcraft in his looks,
And fuck-all in his promises.
Seems ah win again.

She's a pro with the cards.

RAMSAY
Who was he? Some punter?

GRACE
Paid badly.
He'd tell me... Lots o' things.
Said he'd marry me.
But he loved his sonnets, and he loved the sound of his voice...
Sure you want to give me all this money?

RAMSAY
You've changed ma luck.
Ah'll write you sonnets.

GRACE
What use are they?

DEFOE comes in.

RAMSAY
Can't stay away, eh?
He's spruced up now, eh Grace?
Join our cards?

DEFOE
I won't hand your lady my money.

GRACE

Everyone does in the end.

RAMSAY

What d'you say to those lords?
Their faces were white when you left.

DEFOE

Swapped pleasantries.

RAMSAY

Ah spied a letter.
You're intriguing, Mr Defoe.
What do you make of him, Grace?

GRACE

He's sly.

RAMSAY

A wandering scribe, at ease on enemy soil,
Spending money like water, knives in his belt,
Giving our politicians the heebie-jeebies.

GRACE

He's an English spy.

RAMSAY

Nailed it.

DEFOE impassively stares at them.

RAMSAY
Kidding, man!
Take a drink!
Macdonald, bring whisky!
Happily ah'll take an Englishman's money.

He deals DEFOE cards.

DEFOE
Tell me of Scotland.

RAMSAY
Ye behold its glory!
Proudest nation on Earth.
Finest people – pride, eloquence – eh, Macdonald?!

MACDONALD
Go fuck yerself, Ramsay!

RAMSAY
Bring our whisky, ya swindler!

DEFOE
Your politicians seek Union with England.

RAMSAY
Never happen.
How can ye join fire and ice?
Our leaders protect their nation.
Mob would string them up otherwise.

The EARL OF SEAFIELD and EARL OF STAIR enter.

SEAFIELD
Can't believe we're here again.
I was shitting all night after those oysters.

STAIR
The least obvious place.

SEAFIELD
The proprietor should be hanged.

STAIR
All in good time.

SEAFIELD
You told him to come?

STAIR
Request, Seafield. One requests Dukes, never tells them.
They never remember anyway.

SEAFIELD
And is he willing?

STAIR
He sniffs wealth and privilege. Once they're on offer,
The swiftest bloodhound in the kingdom has nothing on
him.
Hope you had no plans this evening.

SEAFIELD
Why?

STAIR
He'll expect us to drink with him.
Think of your promised Marquisate.

Enter the DUKE OF QUEENSBERRY, ostentatiously, as he does everything. The premiere peer of the realm is large in stature, eminently aware of his importance, drunken, irreverent and unimpressed.

QUEENSBERRY
Dear Christ.
The fuck is this, Stair?

STAIR
A place to talk, Your Grace.

QUEENSBERRY
Use ma bloody castle.

STAIR
Anonymity. No-one will disturb us here.

QUEENSBERRY
Nae wonder – are those rats?

STAIR
The authentic Edinburgh experience.

QUEENSBERRY

We'll catch fucking typhoid.

Own half the Borders – castle walls six feet thick and you want tae meet here?

Cancelled an appointment. Rosie Rose.

Only hooker in this fuck-ugly town free from syphilis.

SEAFIELD

We appreciate your time and vow to be swift.

STAIR

I would emphasise the secrecy of this meeting.

QUEENSBERRY

Don't want folk knowing where yer sticky mitts have been?

STAIR

Better for us all. Discreet.

RAMSAY barges over –

RAMSAY

S'cuse me Gentlemen, my lords –

Forgive me, are you the Duke of Queensberry?

QUEENSBERRY, recognising a fan, grows an official smile.

QUEENSBERRY

Indeed I am.

RAMSAY

It's an honour sir, your Grace, an honour...

He announces to the whole pub –

RAMSAY

Ladies, Gentlemen, would you believe it,
The esteemed Duke of Queensberry has graced us with his presence!!

QUEENSBERRY turns gracious statesman, waves.

RAMSAY

Our truest patriot – a champion for desperate times!
The English Parliament seek Union.
But our noble protector flings back their offer!
A Hercules for our time!

QUEENSBERRY

Touched, honoured.

RAMSAY

What you doing in a hole like this?

QUEENSBERRY considers him.

QUEENSBERRY

What's yer name, laddie?

RAMSAY
Ramsay, Allan Ramsay, sir.

QUEENSBERRY
What d'ya do with yourself, Ramsay?

RAMSAY
A writer, Your Grace. Poems, pamphlets –

QUEENSBERRY
Poetry, eh? Bet you know some limericks!

RAMSAY
"There was a young man named Runt,
Whose wife possessed an enormous –"

SEAFIELD
Is this important??

QUEENSBERRY
"She slipped on the stair –"

SEAFIELD
Your Grace –

RAMSAY
"With a bucket of pears –"

STAIR
Queensberry!!

QUEENSBERRY
...Forgetting maself, Ramsay.

RAMSAY
How can ah support your Grace?
Political tracts, victory songs?!

QUEENSBERRY
Grateful, laddie, grateful, a wee bit busy the now –

RAMSAY
Who're yer fellow patriots?

QUEENSBERRY
These rascals?!

STAIR
Careful...

QUEENSBERRY
Discretion, Ramsay.
Our mission demands secrecy.
In this room tonight, Ramsay, we do great deeds. Great deeds!

RAMSAY
Aye?!

QUEENSBERRY

Tonight words become acts,
Myths become legend!

RAMSAY

Myths, your Grace?!

QUEENSBERRY

In this room, Gentlemen,
We chart, for our great nation, a glorious future!

SEAFIELD

Oh Christ –

QUEENSBERRY

We turn the page of history!
Embrace our destiny!
Marching onwards, heads held high!
My Brothers!
We shall be unceasing! Unswerving!
In our efforts to drive Scotland –
THIS GLORIOUS COUNTRY –
Onwards to the new MAGNIFICENT future
BY THE BLOOD OF OUR ANCESTORS
Her Rightful Place Among Equals
in the Proud Dawn of this New Century!!!!!!!!!!!!!!

Pub celebrates – drinks spilt, tankards thrown – they love this shit. QUEENSBERRY, smiling grandly, looks benignly upon his flock.

RAMSAY
He's immortal!

GRACE
He's hammered!

RAMSAY
A Cicero for our times!
A Cicero!

GRACE
Arm wrestle!

RAMSAY
Eh?

GRACE
Wrestle me! I'll destroy y'all!

RAMSAY steps up. They lock arms.

RAMSAY
What's the prize?

GRACE
Yer no shagging me!

*RAMSAY is surprised and GRACE takes advantage,
slamming his arm down.*

RAMSAY
Referee!

GRACE
Winner!

RAMSAY
Best of 3.

They lock arms again. A struggle, then RAMSAY pins her arm down to the table.

RAMSAY
I ask again.

GRACE
What?

RAMSAY
You. One night.

GRACE
Ah said no shagging –

RAMSAY
Out of hours you.
For one night yer no whore – you just spend it with me.
Deal?

GRACE considers, nods – in a flash goes for the slamdown. But RAMSAY is waiting, he uses her weight against her, pinning her to the table...

RAMSAY
Ah caught you, Diana. Yer mine.

GRACE
Gimme a beer.

RAMSAY goes off to get beer.

A commotion as FAVOUR flies in and engulfs the good DUKE in cuddles.

FAVOUR
Jimmy!!

QUEENSBERRY
Lady Favour!!

FAVOUR
What you doing here?

QUEENSBERRY
Come to see you, lassie!
A revolutionary sister, sharing the burdens of our struggle!

He kisses her drunkenly. Pub cheers again!

QUEENSBERRY
Yer arse is getting fat!

FAVOUR
Cheeky Jimmy!

QUEENSBERRY
Growing as flabby as the National Debt.

MACDONALD
More wine, your Grace?

QUEENSBERRY
Piss-juice! Gimme a beer!
Nunc est bibendum!

*Cheers. MACDONALD hands him a tankard, which he downs
with a flourish.*

QUEENSBERRY
So, Stair. What's got yer britches in a panic?

STAIR
The upcoming Parliamentary Act.

QUEENSBERRY
... Cock-fighting?

SEAFIELD
Passing the motion.

QUEENSBERRY
Nae difficulties in passing motions! Eh Favour? Eh?!

FAVOUR
Naughty Jimmy!

SEAFIELD
Could we grasp the matter in hand –

QUEENSBERRY
Dirty bugger!

STAIR
Queensberry!! Put the fucking goods down and give us your full attention!

Atmosphere shatters.

QUEENSBERRY
Run along, gorgeous.

FAVOUR
See me after?

QUEENSBERRY
Aye lassie, I'll be right up you.

She goes. QUEENSBERRY switches mood.

QUEENSBERRY
Better be fucking incendiary.

STAIR
Your assistance is needed.

SEAFIELD
Will Parliament vote the Act through?

QUEENSBERRY
Crafty Lord Stair must surely ken?

STAIR
Whilst flattered by your opinion of my influence,
I'm well aware of my standing in Parliament.

QUEENSBERRY
Half of 'em want tae string you up.

STAIR
I inspire extreme views –

QUEENSBERRY
Half want you tortured first.

STAIR
You're the most powerful peer of the realm.
Charm, cajoling and bullying will swing the argument.
Will the Act be passed or no?

QUEENSBERRY
Why, The Shite, should I tell you gentlemen?

STAIR
Well...

QUEENSBERRY
Yer minor players in a pissy wee sideshow!
Can you debate with the Whigs, duel with Tories?
Fence rhetoric with England's finest?
You haven't the stamina or skill!
Get on hame, leave politics tae its heroes.
Presently, Stair, I've a whore waiting.

STAIR
Rumours circulate of payment.
Twelve thousand pound. Sterling.
We've a list.

He displays DEFOE'S list.

STAIR
Men and their monies.
Every one of them has confirmed.
Yours is the final name.

QUEENSBERRY takes the list.

QUEENSBERRY
What d'you need?

SEAFIELD

Assurance.

STAIR

In writing.

SEAFIELD

This Act will be passed.

QUEENSBERRY

What makes you think it won't?
Listen, the English had a chat.
Yon Kit Kat club – they wield the power – Whigs, thinkers,
hermaphrodites –

STAIR and SEAFILED query –

QUEENSBERRY

More common than you think.
Shaftesbury, Alexander Pope, there were rumours about
James VII...

STAIR

What about them?
The Kit Kat club?!

QUEENSBERRY

Plans are in motion.
On both sides of the border we subdue the dissenters,
Unite the island, expand the economy,

Handsomely reward the most deserving.

And we *deserve* rewards!

Four fucking years of traipsing between here and London,
Shouldering this country's weight.

A saddle-blistered arse that's seen more action than Favour there.

Tortuous mental aerobics with sadistic Robbie fucking Harley.

Too much is at stake.

Fear not, Lord Stair, when titles are handed out, ye'll have yer reward.

SEAFIELD

What about Hamilton?

He'll swing the undecided.

QUEENSBERRY

Jim Hamilton's a preening playboy.

His rhetoric's empty – there's dirt on Hamilton would make a whore blush.

Grubby politics are beneath him.

SEAFIELD

You're sure?

QUEENSBERRY

Soon as he feels which way the winds blowing, he'll fall in line.

And the wind, gentlemen, is blowing oot ma arse

And all the way tae the filthiest slags in Southwark!

MACDONALD brings him another drink –

MACDONALD
On the house, your Grace.

QUEENSBERRY
God love this country!
Beautiful bastards, I love you all!

RAMSAY
3 cheers for the jolly Duke! Hip hip!

WHOLE PUB
Hurray!

RAMSAY
Hip hip!

WHOLE PUB
Hurray!

RAMSAY
Hip *HIP*!

WHOLE PUB
Hurray!!

QUEENSBERRY
Touched! Blessed! Finest on God's earth.

He brings out his purse, tosses coins to the crowd. Punters scramble feverishly, including GRACE. Among the coins she finds STAIR's list!

STAIR and SEAFIELD realise it's time to leave.

STAIR
Our presence is demanded elsewhere.
Mind this conversation.

QUEENSBERRY
You'll get yours, Stair.
All the titles and sluts you can get yer tongue round.
Stick around lads, it's gonnae be a riot!

SEAFIELD
Duty calls.

QUEENSBERRY
Look at em!
Saltiest bastards of the earth!
God loves a sinner, lads! Cos look at the fucking riches He's left me!

Cheers! STAIR and SEAFIELD leave.

RAMSAY
Gie us a song!

QUEENSBERRY

Delighted!

> "Oh I once had a girl named young Flora May,
> She took up the pox in a serious way,
> When I dipped ma wick in her under the clock,
> Ma face turned bright green and so did ma cock!!
> Too-ra loo! Too-ra lay!
> And it's: choose your whore well boys, then hammer
> away!!"

Applause. More drinking.

RAMSAY

How's it feel?

GRACE

Ah've missed a hundred offers.

RAMSAY

You look stunning.
It could be like this.
Ma writing will pay our way.
Ah'm a herald for our times. A prophet.

GRACE

What d'you prophesise fer me?

RAMSAY

Immortality.

Grandly, FAVOUR arrives dressed as a cavalier - long leather boots and a large flamboyant hat. She makes her way to QUEENSBERRY who ogles appreciatively.

QUEENSBERRY
Rag me sideways! Lady Favour!

FAVOUR
You called?

QUEENSBERRY
The fairest of them all!

FAVOUR
What've you got for me Jimmy?

QUEENSBERRY
A cock as hard as iron, Favour.
Sing wi me!

> "Oh I once had a whore named old Mother Mogs,
> As fat as a barrel and smelt of the dogs,
> When she hiked her skirts up, right up tae her chin,
> It took me an hour tae feel it go in!
> Too-ra loo!! Too-ra lay!!
> And it's: choose your whore well boys, then hammer
> away!!"

Pub is raucous. FAVOUR plumps herself down in the DUKE'S lap. Flushed with drink GRACE jumps up on a table.

GRACE
Another verse your Grace!

> "Oh there once was a girl named young Lady Favour,
> As quick with her tongue as any men savoured,
> When they dropped their britches and let her start work,
> It was barely a breath 'til she'd make them jerk!
> Too-ra loo!! Too-ra lay!!
> And it's: choose your whore well boys then hammer away!!"

Cheers. GRACE curtsies.

GRACE
A toast!
Gentlemen. Ladies.

QUEENSBERRY
Join us, Grace?!

GRACE
No, Your Grace, not tonight.
Tonight I am called Diana!

She curtsies and downs another shot – falls off the table – RAMSAY rushes to her – she hugs him fiercely and lands a smacking kiss on his lips – he kisses her back, passionately – picks her up in his arms and carries her out. Pub carries on. QUEENSBERRY snogs the face off his whore cavalier...

London.

Luxurious apartments in the newly established Bank of England. One wall still needs finishing. A picture of LORD HALIFAX sits on the floor needing hanging.

ROBERT WALPOLE, a young, fast-rising politician sits with WILLIAM CONGREVE, a trendy, successful playwright. Both Whigs, both members of the highly influential Kit Cat club, both governors of this new bank. Languidly, they play cards.

WALPOLE
Congreve. Are three queens good?

CONGREVE
'Tis commonly agreed, Walpole.

WALPOLE
Oh.
Not that I possess them of course.
Is it your turn?

CONGREVE
No.

WALPOLE considers his hand.

WALPOLE
Heard about Wren?
They turned down his plans for Westminster.

CONGREVE
He will price himself out of the market.

WALPOLE
He's appealing to the President of the Royal Society.

CONGREVE
Isaac won't help him.

WALPOLE
Why not?

CONGREVE
Because he's a dreadful cunt.

Silence. WALPOLE considers playing a hand, then withdraws.

WALPOLE
Ever since the knighthood he's been throwing his weight around.

CONGREVE
The privilege of Presidency.

WALPOLE

Of Isaac Newton. They're too scared to choose anyone else.

Silence.

WALPOLE

Any new plays?

CONGREVE

No.

WALPOLE

Awaiting inspiration? The Muse to guide your hand?

CONGREVE

Just can't be arsed.

Silence. With a flourish, WALPOLE finally plays his hand.

WALPOLE

Three queens.

CONGREVE plays his.

CONGREVE

Three kings.

WALPOLE

Bugger.

Door opens and LORD HALIFAX enters. Wet, rushed and late.

HALIFAX
Apologies gentlemen, hellish carriage ride –

WALPOLE
Soaking, Charlie!

HALIFAX
Ended up getting out and bloody walking –

CONGREVE
God sends such things to try us.

HALIFAX
But here I am, raring to go!
Who we waiting on?

WALPOLE
Marlborough's on his way, Somers sends apologies, George
–

CONGREVE
George's wife's preggers -

HALIFAX
Again??

CONGREVE
He's prays for a son.

WALPOLE
And a faithful wife!

HALIFAX
Well, sooner we begin.
Now, the reason for this hurried EGM –

CONGREVE
EGM?

HALIFAX
Extraordinary General Meeting.

CONGREVE
Acronym for the day.

WALPOLE
Who's taking minutes?

CONGREVE
I presumed?

HALIFAX
Leave out the poetry this time, Will.

CONGREVE
Have no fear, mere facts and figures.

HALIFAX
As far as I can see, gentlemen –

WALPOLE
Any biscuits?

HALIFAX
As far as –

WALPOLE
Those last week –

HALIFAX
Bob.

WALPOLE
With the coconut –

HALIFAX
Bob!

WALPOLE
Sorry, carry on.

HALIFAX
The only item on the agenda –

CONGREVE
Agendum, Charlie. Singular.

HALIFAX

Agendum. Thank you.

As I was saying – as far as –

The DUKE OF MARLBOROUGH enters. Also soaked, his mood is murderous –

MARLBOROUGH

CUNTS!

WORK-SHY, POX-RIDDEN, BASTARD IRISH *CUNTS!*

CONGREVE

Everything well?

MARLBOROUGH

Fucking carriage drivers!!

HALIFAX

Rough ride?

MARLBOROUGH

Some immigrant Irish *FIEND!*

Charges a fucking *fortune* –

Then in the midst of Covent Garden he dumps me!

Pitches me into the mud and legs it with the fucking carriage!

WALPOLE

Christ!

MARLBOROUGH
Had to fucking walk here!

HALIFAX
Dear me.

MARLBOROUGH
I'll find him! Flush out every Irishman in the city,
Torture the damned shitting lot!

HALIFAX
Right.

MARLBOROUGH
THE IRISH WILL PAY DAMMIT!

CONGREVE
Decimation? Shoot every tenth one?

HALIFAX
Whilst this discussion –

CONGREVE
A la the Roman Legions?

HALIFAX
May we return to the agenda –

CONGREVE
It's –

HALIFAX

Agendum!

The proposed Treaty of Union.

WALPOLE

Oh it's a bloody belter!

A whole country for twenty grand.

CONGREVE

Bugger me. Really?

HALIFAX

Robert Harley assures us the Scots will vote it through.

Once the Treaty passes through both Parliaments...

WALPOLE

Scotland ceases to exist.

CONGREVE

Didn't you live there, John? Serving the old Duke of York?

MARLBOROUGH

Dark. Saturated. Lawless.

Locals completely wild.

Hunt in packs – burning, fucking, drinking everything in sight.

That's just the women.

Hordes of devil children mob the streets.

Ghastly.

WALPOLE
And they wear skirts?

MARLBOROUGH
Highlanders! Barely human.
Terrific fighters – terrify the French.
Used em in Flanders - keep em on chains, starve em,
y'know?
Let em loose at night.

CONGREVE
Hang on – the Scots simply give their country away?

HALIFAX
Well, we just… offered money…

CONGREVE
Have they no loyalty? No national pride?

HALIFAX
… Not really.

CONGREVE
Who would sell out his country?

HALIFAX
We have a list.
They retain their system of law, church… awful cuisine…
Usual propaganda's coming in.
Crop failure, famine, riots…

MARLBOROUGH

Damned ridiculous! Can't *buy* countries!
Gotta *conquer* em!

HALIFAX

John –

CONGREVE

Take the army to Scotland!

MARLBOROUGH

There's an idea!

CONGREVE

Burn and pillage!

MARLBOROUGH

Take the Guards – they're owed a holiday –

HALIFAX

There will be no –

MARLBOROUGH

Edinburgh by morning, Dundee the afternoon –

CONGREVE

Glasgow?

MARLBOROUGH

No, no – they're insane –

HALIFAX
NO ONE'S GOING TO CONQUER SCOTLAND!
It comes for free!

WALPOLE
Actually twenty thousand –

HALIFAX
But we have it!
That's the point of this meeting!
That's what we debate!
No more invasion talk!

MARLBOROUGH
Offer to do a favour...
Spat back in yer face...
Dunno why I bother –

HALIFAX stands abruptly, collects his things, marches out.

A stunned silence.

WALPOLE
What was...?

CONGREVE
I believe we upset Charlie with our military proposition.

MARLBOROUGH
Just a ruddy idea...

CONGREVE

His first meeting as Chairman – he wanted it to go well...

MARLBOROUGH

Shouldn't be so damned sensitive.

Gotta wonder about a chap...

Ever since the affair with that dwarf actress...

WALPOLE

Shall I pop out for biscuits?

Door opens and HALIFAX comes back in. In silence he takes off his coat, takes his chair again. Rearranges his papers.

HALIFAX

Apologies, gentlemen.

WALPOLE/CONGREVE

No, no!

HALIFAX

Sometimes...

WALPOLE/CONGREVE

Yes, yes!

HALIFAX

Where was I?

CONGREVE
The agendum, Charlie.

HALIFAX
Yes. So. Ah-hem.
As the legal custodians of the Bank of England –

WALPOLE
We tell bloody Parliament what to do.

HALIFAX
Of course we gain all Scotland's assets –

CONGREVE
Hang on. What about the Bank of Scotland?

HALIFAX
Yes?

CONGREVE
It's bankrupt. Indebted.

HALIFAX
When created in 1695, the directors raised a whopping
£1,200,000...

WALPOLE
Sweet Nellie's buttocks...

CONGREVE
Which was largely lost in their Darien disaster.

HALIFAX
What's lost may be regained.

CONGREVE
Broken banks are an unwise investment, Charlie.
Calamity breeds calamity.
"Tis the way of the world."

WALPOLE
Touché!

HALIFAX
The point is, Will, the bloody point is –

There's a knock at the door. This surprises them.

HALIFAX
Are we expecting guests?
Who knows we're here?

Another knock.

WALPOLE
Someone bloody answer!

More knocking.

WALPOLE answers the door.

After a moment he returns, with another man.

WALPOLE
Gentlemen, we are graced by a distinguished visitor.
Allow me to present: Robert Harley.

HALIFAX
What??
Who invited *HIM*?

Eyes turn to MARLBOROUGH.

MARLBOROUGH
Thought he'd like to come along?

HALIFAX
This was OUR meeting! MY agenda!
Suppose he wants to be on the board too?

HARLEY
No wish to interrupt proceedings, merely observe.

MARLBOROUGH
He knows about Scotland. Being Secretary for the North.

HALIFAX
Then tell us.

HARLEY
What?

HALIFAX
What don't we know.

HARLEY
That's not for me to say.

HALIFAX
But... You're privileged. The ear of the Queen.

HARLEY
My ignorance of State affairs matches your own.

WALPOLE
What they got?

HARLEY
I'm sorry?

WALPOLE
The Scots – gold? Cotton? Sugar?
Women??

MARLBOROUGH
No, no – vixens! Banshees!

WALPOLE
So what do we get out of it?

HALIFAX
A whole new country, Bob!

WALPOLE
But what's *in* it?

HALIFAX
Well there's... they have beef –

WALPOLE
My farms cover Norfolk!

HALIFAX
They make lace –

CONGREVE
As do the Dutch – for half the price –

HALIFAX
And they make... they have...

HARLEY
Future trade profits.
Severe taxation.
Men for Marlborough's regiments.
And there's always... whisky.

HALIFAX
I propose a vote.
All those in favour of the Treaty?

Four hands are raised.

HALIFAX
Motion passed.

HARLEY
Her Majesty shall be advised accordingly.

MARLBOROUGH
Sarah does it best. Usually with treacle scones.

HALIFAX
How are the minutes coming, Will?

CONGREVE
My pen is flowing faster than my wit.

HALIFAX
Then unless there's anything else, I conclude this meeting.

WALPOLE
Went awfully well, Charlie.
Terrific job.

HALIFAX
Thanks, Bob.
Getting to grips with the role.

HARLEY
Lord Halifax. I left you my carriage. Travel safely.

HALIFAX

Right!
Bid you farewell, gentlemen. Got an appointment.

WALPOLE

Off somewhere nice?

HALIFAX

The theatre. Dryden's new comedy. "Hamlet."

CONGREVE

Rather bloody for a comedy.

HALIFAX

All the best ones are. 'Til Friday.
Harley.

HALIFAX leaves. They watch him go.

CONGREVE

Off to inform his mistress how well it went.
The burdens of authority.

WALPOLE

Pub, gentlemen? Fancy stout and a pie?

MARLBOROUGH

And a strumpet for the digestion!

CONGREVE

Alas, gentlemen, the muse is calling.

The Goddess must be obeyed.

I leave you like a thief in the night.

Satisfied, eminently richer, and a trifle damp.

He leaves.

WALPOLE

His writing's really gone downhill.

John, can I've a word?

MARLBOROUGH

By all means.

...

Harley's alright.

WALPOLE

That favour you promised.

MARLBOROUGH

Found you the brothel.

Eighteen stone, the fattest we could find, a jelly in satin –

WALPOLE

No! No! The OTHER one!

... The Bahamas?

Catherine's getting frumpy I'm not yet a Governor.

MARLBOROUGH

Sarah's like that.

Make one mistake – one tiny mistake.

Once shot her hamster.

Tidying the desk and the fucker ran across it.

Blew it to smithereens.

Never hear the end of it.

HARLEY

... Tidying your desk?

WALPOLE

If you could have a word.

MARLBOROUGH

Yes, yes, first thing tomorrow.

WALPOLE

Perhaps this handing out of countries will put

Her Majesty in a generous frame of mind?

MARLBOROUGH

Who knows?

Can never tell what goes on in her mind.

Always detached. Like a butter knife.

Odd creatures, women.

Beat.

HARLEY

The Queen will be delighted with this evening's events.

Funds needed for the next war.

The noble Duke has itchy campaigning feet.

MARLBOROUGH

Too many damned French in the world.

HARLEY

And if the Scots will not come by peaceful means...

English ambition expands at every frontier.

Including the Caribbean,

Where Her Majesty needs leaders of fortitude and vision.

Pirates operate out of some islands she's particularly keen on...

WALPOLE

Then they need to go.

HARLEY

Meeting the Queen tomorrow.

She does love good news.

Shall we step into the night, gentlemen?

Beer is the perfect tonic for a rainy evening.

And women of negotiable affection. I know a jolly wee place.

They leave.

Scene 5   Ramsay's Lodging

The morning after.

ALLAN RAMSAY'S meagre lodging. GRACE lies asleep.
Clothes scatter the floor. RAMSAY sits, quill in hand, writing
intently.

GRACE stirs. Wakes. Stretches, unsure where she is. She sees
him.

GRACE
Dear Christ. Day already?
Ma head's been split open.
What you doing?

RAMSAY
Capturing you, just as you are. Were.
Your morning bed.

GRACE gets up, stretches. He grabs a blanket.

RAMSAY
Should be draped. Like a Vestal Virgin.

GRACE
No virgin. Not since ah was 9.
Ma head. Lord.
Did we drink last night?

RAMSAY
Like heathens.

GRACE
Feel like Jimmy Queensberry's ragged me sideways.

RAMSAY
He banged a cavalier instead.

GRACE
His shindigs are the best.
'Til morning comes and you have tae heave his carcass off you.

RAMSAY
You were singing.

GRACE
Christ!

She sees his writing.

RAMSAY
Poetry.

GRACE
Cannae read.

RAMSAY

Ah'll teach you.

From Catullus to Shakespeare.

GRACE

Ah'm a slow learner. Unless it's shagging.

What? You don't like that?

Read me your poem.

RAMSAY

When it's published.

Yer a Princess this morning.

Ah'll give you palaces.

Beat.

GRACE

What about you? When did you lose it?

RAMSAY

You make it sound vulgar.

GRACE

Go on. Who took your cherry?

RAMSAY goes back to writing.

GRACE
You're ashamed?
Tell me.
Who first plucked you?

RAMSAY
You did.

Beat.

GRACE
How d'you last this long?
Lassies'd be gagging for you.

RAMSAY
Clearly not.

GRACE
Had three abortions by your age.

RAMSAY
Don't talk like that.

GRACE
Don't like how ah talk?

RAMSAY
Ah love how...
Stay. Stay here.
With me. As my...

GRACE
Your?

RAMSAY
Would you?

GRACE
Would ah?

RAMSAY
If ah asked you?

GRACE
Ah dunno what yer asking me!

RAMSAY
How do you feel?

GRACE
You've high hopes of ma heart, Allan!
D'you no think it was frozen years back?

RAMSAY
Ah'd wager last night it was full of me.

GRACE
Ah was full of you alright –

RAMSAY breaks away.

RAMSAY

You mock everything.

Did you not...?

Last night – the pub – it was deafening.

Defoe's eyeballs were popping out.

"This is your country?!" he kept saying.

Whisky and talking politics with Queensberry.

Our nation's saviour guffawing over ma puns!

GRACE

Be careful of Queensberry –

RAMSAY

He goes to Parliament, fighting fer our future.

GRACE

Politics are dangerous, Allan.

Secrets get ye killed –

RAMSAY

Birling you about. Holding you.

Ah felt 10 foot tall.

Stay.

Stay the rest of the day.

GRACE

You're beautiful.

Ah need tae earn a crust.

Silence.

RAMSAY
How many?

GRACE
Does it matter?

RAMSAY
What do they pay?

GRACE
Allan...

RAMSAY
Ah'll match it.

GRACE
Why d'you waste yer money on me?

RAMSAY
Ah'd loot Heaven tae keep you here.

Silence.

GRACE
Ah'll come by tomorrow.

She's going.

RAMSAY
Grace?

GRACE
Aye?

RAMSAY
How was ah?

GRACE
You were...
Very impressive.

RAMSAY
You're mocking me.

GRACE
Oh Allan, you were sweet.
You *are* sweet.
A spark of fire lighting this cynical old doxie.
Be thinking of you aw day.
Write me more poems.

RAMSAY watches her go. He heads back to his desk. Picks up his quill.

Scene 6   **The Scottish Parliament**

3rd October, 1706.

Magnificent chamber of the Scottish Parliament.

Attending are DUKE OF QUEENSBERRY, EARL OF STAIR and others – supporters of Union. DUKE OF HAMILTON, LORD BELHAVEN oppose them – defenders of Independence.

The EARL OF SEAFIELD, presiding officer, takes charge. It's been a long session.

SEAFIELD
One item remains for the day.
A Treaty, bearing the seal of our Sovereign,
Comes before us for debate.
Commissioners from both this Parliament and Westminster,
Have wrestled with its complexities.
But time for private consideration has passed.
Today we publicly debate.
Who shall open proceedings?
The Earl of Stair.

STAIR
My lords. Gentlemen.
Harsh, harsh times continue to dwell.
Grey clouds shroud the horizon.
Storms lash our capital, despair stalks the streets.

Our economy matches the grim weather.

But there is a saving grace.

An old solution, proffered several times before.

But every previous incarnation, culminating in the proposed Union Act of 1689,

Has been a disaster.

Mangled in wording, biased, poorly presented –

Rightly, each has been voted down by this Parliament.

LORD

Hear, hear!

STAIR

Now we have a new proposal.

Carefully conceived,

Striking the balance between aspiration and practicality.

31 Commissioners representing our country – and this Parliament –

Have, for years, negotiated with their English counterparts,

Battling for the best deal for Scotland.

Their tribulations and talents culminate in this document.

New ground is trodden. History beckons.

I urge you, my lords; for the sake of our country,

For the salvation of our economy, and for our descendants,

Vote the Treaty of the Act of Union to be passed.

Thus we truly civilise our country, from Lowland to Highland.

Cheers from the Unionist faction.

SEAFIELD
The floor is open.

JAMES, DUKE OF HAMILTON appears. Dashing and handsome, a man of nous and charisma, he's a polished politician and enemy of STAIR'S.

SEAFIELD
His Grace, the Duke of Hamilton.

HAMILTON
Silken words, Lord Stair.
Dark days indeed fall upon us.
Recession smashes our markets, hunger claws our people.
Our one great hope for colonial power – Darien – has failed.
Parliament descends into factions, riven by jealousy,
scrabbling for power.
100 of our 223 members belong to the Court Party –
Whose loyalty is more to the English Whig administration,
Than the people of Scotland –

SEAFIELD
Thank you, Your Grace –

HAMILTON
Scots have fought tooth and claw for independence.
We withstood Longshanks, Henry VIII, Cromwell.
And when our old English enemies ran out of royalty,
It was to us they turned for a monarch!
Robert Bruce is jigging in heaven,

Now his descendant occupies the English throne.

We are an independent race, Lords.

We take pride in our Parliament,

Our Law, Church, trade, culture.

True, we share a sovereign with England,

But remember from whose bloodline she descends.

And if we so wish, we may choose our own heir to Queen Anne.

Her father had another child in lawful wedlock.

A son.

LORD

Jacobite!

HAMILTON

Nationalist, my lord!

My forefathers defended our independence,

And I continue a proud tradition.

English monarchs ever sought to conquer us, by war or diplomacy.

But every attempt to amalgamate our separate countries has failed.

Two nations.

Like oil and water, they cannot mix.

This Treaty must meet the fate of its predecessors.

Honour the commitments of your ancestors,

And vote it down.

Thunderous applause.

STAIR

Two nations.

One language. One island.

A Union of Crowns.

Prosperity, economic stability, and imperial ambitions

Can only be achieved by a single, strong, united Parliament!

SEAFIELD

Lord Belhaven.

BELHAVEN

Then base it in Edinburgh!

Drag yon English MP's up here!

Queensberry, was that even an option?

We are discussing a conquest!

SEAFIELD

Order!

BELHAVEN

By our greatest rival and bitterest enemy –

STAIR

Who offers an olive-branch in our time of trial –

BELHAVEN

Only to bend it to a noose to choke us.

HAMILTON

In the words of Saltoun:

"All of our affairs, since the union of crowns,

Have been managed by the advice of English ministers" –

LORDS

Shame!

HAMILTON

"We have, from that time, appeared to the rest of the world more like a *Conquered Province*, than a free independent people" –

LORDS

Yes! Yes!

HAMILTON

I warn you my lords! I warn you all!

STAIR

Does Hamilton dress like one of the conquered?

HAMILTON

A slave's coat may resemble the garb of his master.

STAIR

Bollocks!

SEAFIELD

Order! Civility shall reign.

Before we debate the Articles of this Treaty,

I deem it prudent to hear from one of the Commissioners

Who has been at the heart of negotiations with the English.

His Grace, the Duke of Queensberry.

To some applause, some boos, QUEENSBERRY takes his place.

QUEENSBERRY

Forgive me, my lords, I am weary...

LORD BELHAVEN

Our Queen's Commissioner exhausts himself nightly with his private cavalier!

QUEENSBERRY

Whilst you consort with roundheads and stable-boys, Lord Belhaven –

SEAFIELD

Your Grace!

QUEENSBERRY

Apologies, Sir.

So disorientated am I from the business of state,

I believed for a moment I was back in the English Parliament.

They are less couth there.

Laughter.

QUEENSBERRY
I am weary, lords.
Night and day, the commissioners have been in session,
Negotiating on your behalf.
A responsibility we bear willingly, gratefully...

BELHAVEN
And financially!

QUEENSBERRY
Would my honourable lord care to swap positions?
Could he joust with English power-brokers?
Would he gamble with Robert Harley, the greatest
politician of the age,
And not lose his shirt, his mind and country?
Perhaps my distinguished friend would treat with Queen
Anne,
Navigating the wily schemes of his monarch?
Perhaps the honourable gentleman would like tae meet me
tomorrow at dawn,
AND FIGHT A DUEL ON THE SLOPES OF *ARTHUR'S
FUCKING SEAT!!*

Silence of a singular sort.

QUEENSBERRY
Session after session I met with the English,
Battling to attain the best possible deal for Scotland.

Every clause has been debated, every benefit scrapped for.
I have lost sleep, money... I am even below my fighting weight...

Laughter.

QUEENSBERRY
Whilst above us hovers the threat of war.
Mistake not, if this Treaty fails, warfare with England is the result.
And would we battle the Duke of Marlborough?
The greatest soldier of our age, who at present,
Slaughters the combined armies of France and Spain?
A man who pimps his own sister to James VII,
Would little prevent his soldiers rampaging our streets,
Massacring our citizens, ransacking our institutions.
My honourable opponents, the Lords Hamilton and Belhaven,
Touchingly talk of Scotland as an ideal.

The fabled dreams of the noble Bruce.
Fantasy.
A dream as broken as our economy.
We are in debt, impoverished, impotent.
How can we protect our citizens?
What assurance may we offer?
Examine well this Treaty, Lords.
At stake is the very existence of our nation.

SEAFIELD

Thank you, Lord Queensberry.

We shall debate each point of the Treaty until satisfaction is achieved.

If not, we shall not hear of it again.

BLACK!

ACT II

Scene 1   **The Saltyre**

November, 1706.

Winter has come and fire burns in the hearth. Still it rains outside.

ALLAN RAMSAY works intently, filling sheaves of paper with his writing.

FAVOUR watches him closely. As does MACDONALD.

FAVOUR
What's this?
All these pages?

She picks up the paper. RAMSAY firmly takes it back.

RAMSAY
A love story.

FAVOUR
Ah! Fiction.

MACDONALD
What's it about?

RAMSAY

The Judgement of Paris.

FAVOUR

What you writing French for?

RAMSAY

Paris from "The Iliad."

He was tasked tae choose the most beautiful goddess.

MACDONALD

What's his options?

RAMSAY

Athena, Zeus's daughter, Goddess of Wisdom.

Hera, wife of Zeus.

Aphrodite, Goddess of love.

MACDONALD

Sounds like you don't want to piss off Zeus.

FAVOUR

Who wins?

RAMSAY

He examines them all.

Finally he gives the golden apple –

MACDONALD

Why's he giving out apples?

RAMSAY

It's the prize.

MACDONALD

They're goddesses and all they get is an apple?

RAMSAY

He awards the apple to Aphrodite.
The only possible choice.

FAVOUR

Yer wasting yer ink. Yer pages will dissolve in the rain.
You see em, floating in the Nor Loch.
Folk's messages, love letters. Turning tae mulch.

RAMSAY

Shouldn't you be shagging someone?

FAVOUR

She'd always a soft spot fer ye.
S'one thing we lose – you become iron – have tae.
But Grace's just got softer.

RAMSAY

Ah don't need your misery.

FAVOUR

Can this feed weans?
3 boys with bottomless stomachs.
Had more, but they died.

Oh Death dwells right close.

You feel his breath.

And if yer really unloved, he'll leave you here.

Ah've mouths tae feed. And babes tae care fer.

She pecks him on the cheek.

FAVOUR

It's aw an endless sea of shite, Allan.

You'll learn.

RAMSAY

Ah inhabit a brighter world.

A new dawn, Favour.

The country's awakening.

Door opens and GRACE comes in. RAMSAY leaps to her –

RAMSAY

Ah cracked it, Grace!

GRACE

Which?

RAMSAY

Paris and his Goddesses.

After betrayal, reconciliation.

Pin folk tae the edge of their seats, then lift them tae the Gods!

Yer soaking!

GRACE

Ma carriages are aw getting mended.

Could murder a drink.

RAMSAY pours her whisky. She necks it.

GRACE

The Canongate's a muddy sea.

The shite's running in rivers down the closes.

Rats chase cats.

FAVOUR

But jinglin' Jim Hamilton pays well!

RAMSAY

Hamilton?

FAVOUR

Wealthiest benefactor in town.

RAMSAY

D'you want tae hear something?

GRACE

Something?

RAMSAY

Something of mine.

GRACE

Only if it features me, Allan.

RAMSAY

Of course!
Ah'm adapting the story.
Greek Goddesses are mighty fine,
But our Edinburgh lassies take the apple.
Listen!

He reads from his manuscript.

RAMSAY

"The tawny nymph, on scorching plains,
May use the aid of gems and paint,
Deck with brocade and Tyrian stains
Features of ruder form and taint:
What Caledonian ladies wear,
Or from the lint or woollen twine,
Adorn'd by all their sweets, appear
Whate'er we can imagine fine."

GRACE

No bad, Ramsay, no bad –

RAMSAY

"T'adore dear Grace who can cease?" –

GRACE

You write of me, my lord?

RAMSAY

Thy looks, lady, inspire the Gods!
Eh, Macdonald?
Ain't these damsels the world's finest?

MACDONALD

Princesses all!

RAMSAY

"T'adore dear Grace who can cease?
Her active charms our praise demand,
Clad in a mantua, from the fleece
Spun by her own delightful hand."

"Who can behold Grace's eyes,
Her breast, her cheek, and snowy arms,
And mind what artists can devise
To rival more superior charms?"

FAVOUR

Everybody!
Everyone's seen her breasts, her *snowy arms* –

RAMSAY

Poetry, Favour.
You widnae understand.

FAVOUR

Sounds like whoring tae me.

GRACE
How much have you written?

RAMSAY
Seven verses.

FAVOUR
Punters will definitely be needing a shag before ye finish.

RAMSAY
We must abandon these Philistines, Grace.
Ah'll find a patron who appreciates.
Queensberry will love this.

MACDONALD
The fat Duke journeyed south.
Her Majesty recalled the Commissioners.

RAMSAY
Queensberry fights fer our freedom!

MACDONALD
Seems tae involve a lot of drinking.

GRACE
Any oysters left? Ah'm starving.

RAMSAY
We'll ransack Leith!
Ah'll give ye a boat-load.

GRACE
A dozen is grand, Allan.

RAMSAY
C'mon – ah'll bribe ye with kisses.

GRACE
They cost extra, my lord.

RAMSAY
This wallet is deep!
Ah'll dance ye there on tales of Arcadia!
Leave this dump far behind!

GRACE
And will ye find me a palace too?

RAMSAY
Why wish fer a palace when there's Leith?
Join me, Diana!
We'll turn the locals green with envy!

GRACE takes his arm and they elegantly sweep out.

FAVOUR
He'll ruin her.
Fill her head with dreams.
And vanish when he's grown bored.

MACDONALD

He's a laddie.

Dreams are not our domain.

Should put that in his French story.

Romance of the dreamless poor,

Grinning through disease, drinking themselves to early mass graves.

It'd bring the house down.

No-one'd believe a word of it.

Kensington Palace, London.

DUKE OF QUEENSBERRY sits slumped on a chair, deeply hung over. Perfectly sober, the EARL OF STAIR stalks around the room.

Eventually QUEENSBERRY goes to a bell and rings it. The MASTER appears.

QUEENSBERRY
Wine. Immediately.
Red and cheap.

MASTER
We have a selection –

QUEENSBERRY
Gimme the rankest ye've got.
Hair of the dog man!

MASTER
... You want a dog?

STAIR
Bring him wine immediately.

MASTER
I can recommend a Burgundy –

STAIR

Just stick your hand in the cellar – go!

The MASTER leaves, deeply affronted.

STAIR

Where d'you stay last night?

QUEENSBERRY

God knows.

Woke up wi two of them on me.

Dogs – the lassies had run off with ma cash.

Had to pawn ma rings – buy some clothes.

Cheap English threads. Pish.

STAIR

They gave us rooms in St James's Palace.

Biggest breakfast I've ever had.

Flunkies on call throughout the night.

Fancy working here, Queensberry?

I'm not adverse to basking in this luxury.

Door opens. A figure appears. DANIEL DEFOE.

DEFOE

Gentlemen.

STAIR

You?

DEFOE
Thought I would pay respects.

QUEENSBERRY
Did I drink with you last night?

STAIR
Defoe spies for the English.

QUEENSBERRY
Defoe? The pamphleteer?

STAIR
Traitor.
Switches allegiance faster than a street whore.

DEFOE
Her Majesty generously forgave my misdemeanours.

STAIR
Your saviour, Robert Harley, plucked your from the stocks.

DEFOE
I salute your research.

STAIR
We possess agents as well.

DEFOE

Whose talents have delivered your country to her oldest enemy.

A diplomatic triumph. Destiny bares its fangs.

But... politics. A grubby affair. Best left to politicians.

Do excuse me, my lords.

State affairs to meddle with.

I shall tour your country.

Always good to visit conquered lands.

STAIR

No-one conquered us.

DEFOE

We just did.

A war, centuries old, whose final battle was won by stealth.

STAIR

Spies are expendable.

Beat.

DEFOE

My father was a tallow chandler.

Any idea?

He melted down ox fat to make candles

Which he sold to households of grandees like yourselves.

In hard times, I'd steal it for him.

Amazing where you find fat.

Graveyards. Abattoirs. Aged 7, I bartered with slaughtermen.

STAIR

My heart bleeds.

DEFOE

Seen children burned alive by the Great Fire.

Starved inside prisons.

Princely shoulders I clap and at whores' feet I kneel.

We are all of us on Fortune's Wheel, Stair.

But one thing is clear.

A death knell sounds for your country.

Rung by her lords, and echoed by the Queen's Commissioners.

England owns you.

And if we buy you, shall we not tax you?

And shall we not recklessly fleece you for all you've got?

And once you're bled dry,

We'll take your industries, your culture, your history,

And make them ours.

English garrisons from Edinburgh to Inverness.

Boundaries will be redrawn. Your language will disappear.

There's your conquest, Lords!

You proud masters of politics!

Your poor citizens would despair.

He leaves with a flourish.

STAIR

That lad would be none the worse for a good hanging.

QUEENSBERRY retches.

STAIR

Dear gods!
Why d'you drink so much?

QUEENSBERRY

Must be the fucking climate.

STAIR

Last thing we need is you vomiting over our Sovereign.
Assemble your scattered wits.
Got the speech?
...
The speech? The message from Parliament??

QUEENSBERRY

Must've misplaced it.

STAIR

Then what will you say?

QUEENSBERRY shrugs.

STAIR

Queensberry, this is crucial!
You've mislaid the Parliamentary mail!

QUEENSBERRY
You do it.

STAIR
Me??

QUEENSBERRY
Aye, why no?

STAIR
I HAVEN'T A CLUE WHAT THE MESSAGE WAS!!
What the fuck are we going to do??

QUEENSBERRY
Busk it.

The MASTER appears through the double doors.

MASTER
Her Majesty will see you now.

STAIR
Oh Christ!

QUEENSBERRY
About bloody time, sunshine!
Stair. Prepare to meet thy sovereign.

We move to...

The MASTER brings QUEENSBERRY and STAIR into the magnificent reception chamber.

QUEEN ANNE is listening to SARAH CHURCHILL, who is in full flow. QUEEN ANNE cradles a doll.

SARAH
Emeralds, darling??
Bloody *emeralds??*
With your complexion?
May as well dress with cabbage!

QUEEN ANNE
A gift from the Duke of Brunswick –

SARAH
I left the perfect jewels. Yet Annie decides to find her own accoutrements!

QUEEN ANNE
Emeralds we prefer to sapphires –

SARAH
I prefer St James' Palace to this old dump yet suffer your questionable taste!

QUEEN ANNE
May the Queen not dress herself?

SARAH

Observe the results!

How may any true friend remain silent,

When their dearest soul resembles a painted sow?!

MASTER

Your Majesty —

SARAH

As for policy, why do we war with the French?

QUEEN ANNE

Thought Marlborough wished it?

The bloodbath at Ramillies?

SARAH

That was last summer!

He's sick of slogging through Belgian mud,

With no reward but stale beer and bunions.

Treat with Louis and we'll call the whole thing off!

Subdue countries closer to home.

Like Scotland.

QUEEN ANNE sits on her throne. Unaware (or uncaring) of her guests, she opens the front of her dress, raises the doll and proceeds to breastfeed.

MASTER

Majesty, you have guests.

QUEEN ANNE sees her visitors. She closes the front of her dress.

MASTER
Allow me to introduce his Grace, the Duke of Queensberry, Marquess of Dumfriesshire, Earl of Drumlanrig and Sanquhar –

SARAH
Well?!

Beat.

MASTER
Viscount of Nith, Tothorwald and Ross –

SARAH
May Johnnie to declare a truce?

MASTER
Lord Douglas of Kinmount –

SARAH
Oh Willie, do be quiet!
Cannot think with you prattling on!

QUEEN ANNE
You were saying, Willie?

MASTER
... and Lord Privy Seal of Scotland.

QUEEN ANNE
Broad shoulders for so many titles.

QUEENSBERRY
Majesty.
We bring greetings from the Scottish Parliament –

SARAH
Annie! Do not ignore me!

QUEEN ANNE
Our audience is ended for today, your Grace.

Beat.

SARAH
An insult too far, your Majesty.
Our kind requests – rudely ignored.

QUEEN ANNE
Sarah, don't be like this.

SARAH
Difficult to fathom her Majesty's foolishness –

QUEEN ANNE
What would you have me do?

SARAH

Heed our patient advice!
Reign! Dispense wisdom like Solomon!
Not cower behind skirts,
Wallowing in self-pity and fear!

QUEEN ANNE

Unkind, Sarah!

SARAH

We have endured loss, my darling!
My son perished, and I wept an ocean's tears,
But life sweeps ever onward.

QUEEN ANNE

Every one of them, Sarah! All gone!

SARAH

Then look to thyself.
When the Queen loses her entire flock,
The fault does not lie with God.
Upon the Marlborough rock your state is founded.
Your majesty basks in our embrace.
Ever-willing, ever-kind-hearted!
When Annie comes crying that all the world despises her –
Parliament, the commons, God himself –
Whose honey words flow to content her?
Harsh is the judgement you pass over those who love you.

QUEEN ANNE
My dear darling, I am sorry!

SARAH
Apologies dance too easily on our sovereign's tongue,
She should examine her blunders instead.
I leave Her Majesty with her simple Scots playfellows.
At Blenheim I await your contrition.

She bows again, and sweeps magnificently out.

QUEEN ANNE
Willie...

MASTER
Have strength, Majesty —

QUEEN ANNE
She rebuked me.

MASTER
We shall pacify her.
I will send jewellery.

QUEEN ANNE
Not emeralds.

MASTER
Perhaps that tea salesman?

QUEEN ANNE

Wait.

She presumes too much.

Let her consider her harsh words.

MASTER

Certainly, Ma'am.

And now...

Your Commissioners from Scotland.

QUEEN ANNE

What news, my lords?

QUEENSBERRY turns on the charm.

QUEENSBERRY

Only good tidings, Highness.

Our Parliament debates your Union Treaty.

Every clause is scrutinised.

But the outcome is clear.

Scotland will accept. You shall rule a united island.

QUEEN ANNE

The specifics?

QUEENSBERRY

Too tedious to list, Majesty.

But victory is assured.

QUEEN ANNE
Jolly good.
Care to join me for tea?

QUEENSBERRY
Be honoured, Ma'am.

QUEEN ANNE
Who's your accomplice?

QUEENSBERRY
Your Majesty, may I present John Dalrymple, the Earl of Stair.

STAIR bows.

QUEEN ANNE
Stair. Yes.

QUEENSBERRY
Loyal patriot and promoter of Union, Ma'am.

QUEEN ANNE
Ordered Glencoe, I believe?
All those people slaughtered in the snow.

STAIR
Your Majesty's enemies. Rebels.

QUEEN ANNE
Mothers. Children...

MASTER
No, Your Majesty –

QUEEN ANNE
Sugar?
Do, it's lovely.

STAIR
Two, then.

QUEEN ANNE
See my baby?
Isn't she gorgeous?

STAIR & QUEENSBERRY examine the doll.

QUEENSBERRY
Quite gorgeous, Ma'am.

QUEEN ANNE
Willie wants me to abandon her, don't you, Willie?
But who else shall I breast feed?
They all keep dying on me, y'see.
Berthed in me all those months, sucking me dry.
I spit them out like lemon pips – still they shuffle off.
Take the oldest one. Charles.

MASTER
William, Ma'am.

QUEEN ANNE
William.
They had to drag him out with pincers.
Always sick. Reached 11 and died of shock.

MASTER
Pneumonia, Majesty.

QUEEN ANNE
Named him after my brother-in-law.
King William –

QUEENSBERRY
May he rest in peace –

QUEEN ANNE
 – Was an arse bandit.

MASTER
Ma'am –

QUEEN ANNE
He kept a harem.
All these common boys, greasy, flea-ridden paupers,
Greedy for royal cock. Willie's Brigade.

Dressed them in lace and screwed them in the State
Apartments.
Not a nancy are you, Lord Stair?

STAIR
No, Your Majesty.

QUEEN ANNE
Palaces are crawling with them.
Everywhere I go. Blenheim. Kensington.
Dressing as duchesses and buggering the young grooms.
Still, perhaps it's different in your country. My country.
Should I visit, Stair?

STAIR
Certainly, Majesty.

QUEEN ANNE
What does one do there?

STAIR
Same as here. Ride. Shoot. Tax.

QUEEN ANNE
Any beverages? I drink tea.
Gallons of it. Piss like a fountain.

QUEENSBERRY

Whisky, Ma'am.

Bit stronger than tea.

Got some here, actually.

QUEEN ANNE

May one taste?

MASTER

Majesty! Perhaps a bad idea?

QUEEN ANNE considers.

She takes a slug of the flask QUEENSBERRY offers her. She coughs.

QUEEN ANNE

Quite a... quite a kick...

QUEENSBERRY

Warms the cockles.

QUEEN ANNE

Tastes like... tastes *like*...

QUEENSBERRY

Nectar?

STAIR

Poison?

QUEEN ANNE
Burnt...

QUEENSBERRY
Peat soil?!

QUEEN ANNE
Frenchmen!
Johnnie Marlborough shot some prisoners at the Tower,
Had them cremated. The smell hung on the air for weeks.

QUEENSBERRY
Taste some more, Ma'am.

QUEEN ANNE takes another sip.

QUEENSBERRY
No, you've got tae knock it back! In a wunner!

QUEENSBERRY collects some glasses, pours out measures.
QUEEN ANNE is handed a shot. She hesitates then bravely
knocks it back.

QUEEN ANNE
Crikey.

QUEENSBERRY
C'mon, let's do another –

He fills 3 glasses, hands them round –

QUEENSBERRY
Stair! A toast!

STAIR
Our Gracious Sovereign, Anne.
Her continuing health.

QUEENSBERRY
Och, there's better toasts than that!
Our beauteous sovereign, Anne.
May the bloom be in her cheeks,
The sun on her face, and a stable-boy in —

STAIR
Cheers!

They down the whisky.

QUEENSBERRY
Another!

STAIR
Perhaps enough?

QUEENSBERRY
Bollocks! Let's get pished.

MASTER
Majesty, I really must protest.
The Portuguese Viceroy is due in ten minutes.

QUEEN ANNE
He can wait.
The smelly short-arse.

She giggles.

QUEENSBERRY
That's the spirit, lassie!

MASTER
I fear I must insist, Ma'am.

QUEEN ANNE
Don't be such a bore, Willie!

MASTER
One can't be reeking of – that is, one needs one's faculties –

QUEENSBERRY
Who the hell is this??

QUEEN ANNE
My Master of Household.

QUEENSBERRY
And why, in the name of the wee man, is *he* giving the orders?

QUEEN ANNE
Willie. Leave us.

MASTER
Majesty –

QUEENSBERRY
OUT! G'on, scuttle off ya clown!

The MASTER, affronted, stalks out.

QUEENSBERRY
Gotta learn them, Ma'am, else they start running the show.

QUEEN ANNE
Lord Queensberry – what did I make you?

QUEENSBERRY
Lord High Commissioner for... err...

QUEEN ANNE
No matter.
Tell me, Queensberry, do you know some songs?

QUEENSBERRY assumes the position and regales a filthy song. With actions. QUEEN ANNE necks whisky. STAIR watches on in disgust 'til the end.

> "Her name was Mary Primrose and a buxom wench was she,
> A milkmaid by her trade, with skin that smelt of cheese.

With hair of gold, with breasts sae ripe and skin of ivory,

An appetite that's plumbed the depths of her depravity.

If you should stroll the bonnie banks o' mighty river Clyde,

A milking you might go when buxom Mary opens wide.

A fleece on her back, a bell round her neck, she tinkles when she cums,

And if you hold her nose, then milk erupts from out her bum."

STAIR
Marvellous, Queensberry, perhaps we might –

QUEEN ANNE
Capital, Queensberry!
A veritable delight!

QUEENSBERRY
Plenty more where that came from!

QUEEN ANNE
So many songs feature milkmaids.
Astonishing they spend so much time rutting.
Have you seen my baby?

STAIR carefully hands her the doll.

QUEEN ANNE

My little lamb.

Forgotten half their names.

Georgie had such wind!

Bang on him for hours but he kept burping!

And then, and then, he hiccupped and he couldn't stop –

His tummy writhing in spasms –

Cheeks swelled up – like a hamster –

And then, *then*, the bastard died!

QUEENSBERRY finds this hilarious. They both roar.

QUEEN ANNE

I could kill you.

One raise of this wee little finger.

QUEENSBERRY

How? Poison?

QUEEN ANNE

No – so cowardly – the fucking French do it.

QUEENSBERRY

Beheading!

QUEEN ANNE

Messy. Like childbirth.

Did you meet my little baby? Where is she?

QUEENSBERRY

She crawled off somewhere.

QUEEN ANNE

No, she can't crawl.

QUEENSBERRY

Why not?

QUEEN ANNE

Cos she's a bloody doll!

They roar again. STAIR looks on.

QUEEN ANNE

Did you meet my husband?
Forget what I done with him.
He's *Danish.* Can't touch him.

QUEENSBERRY

But you keep...

QUEEN ANNE

Oh we mate! We fuck like mice.
A new brood every Spring.
Hardly the real thing.

QUEENSBERRY roars again. QUEEN ANNE doesn't.

QUEEN ANNE

Sarah gave me George's miniature in a locket.

Honey blond hair. Blue eyes. Kind.

I was ripe for marriage and Louis XIV of France suggested him.

Protestant. Could have been King of Poland but wouldn't convert.

I waited for... something.

Sarah dried my eyes, and persuaded me to marry.

He wouldn't beat me nor banish her.

Johnnie Churchill brought George across.

There he was. Striding towards me, this tall, blond Immortal.

I fainted and had to be bled.

King William was terribly ashamed.

My eyes were streaming – always watered, since I was a child.

Set the whole court giggling.

We were introduced over Battenberg and tea.

His hair was immaculate and his eyes dark as the moon.

Married in front of 7 monarchs.

That night, before the wedding chamber, I necked brandy with Sarah.

She arranged my hair, my nightgown.

When I reached the wedding chamber that night,

Could hardly walk for shaking.

He was waiting, boots beside the bed, clothes folded neatly.

Took off my nightdress and let my hair fall.

Pulled back the blankets and crept in beside him.

His skin was ice.

I waited. Terrified, my heart...
Finally he sort of rolled onto me, all elbows and knees.
He wiggled until his thing jabbed inside me,
And began rocking rhythmically, eyes searching for mine.
Couldn't meet his gaze.
And then he started gasping and he arched his back,
Pressed against my breasts and went very still.
Rolled back and lay, his breathing stilled.
He rose, put on his boots, and left for a cigar.
I gathered up my nightdress, crept to Sarah's room.
She enfolded me, kissing tears away.
Lay awake the whole night, George's seed dribbled inside.
A vessel for his progeny.
First of the stillborns.

Silence. QUEENSBERRY has fallen unconscious.

QUEEN ANNE
What do you love, Lord Stair?

STAIR
My gloves.
Got them in Shoreditch. Kidskin. The lining's threaded with
gold.

QUEEN ANNE
No Lady Stair waiting for you in Edinburgh?

STAIR
My wife and I spend as much time apart as we are able.

171

My father thought her suitable. I am ever dutiful.
We all have our crosses.

QUEEN ANNE
Not all have to be borne.

STAIR
I mind not the weight.

QUEEN ANNE
And Queensberry? What of his wife?

QUEENSBERRY snores.

STAIR
He has his whores. Little angels of mercy.
His children he infects with their disease.
James, his son is insane. An imbecile.
Could be worse. Could be cuckolding other men's wives.

QUEEN ANNE
You're a singular man, Lord Stair.
Ordering the Glencoe massacre.
Innocents slaughtered in the snow.

STAIR
Everyone dies, Your Majesty.

QUEEN ANNE
My nursemaids are well aware of that, Lord Stair.

STAIR
I did but my duty.

QUEEN ANNE
Children died for your duty.

STAIR
They were better dead.
We rid your realm of traitors and thieves.

QUEEN ANNE
Our audience is at an end.

She rings a bell.

STAIR
King William saw my value.

QUEEN ANNE
I have no place for butchers at my court, Lord Stair.

The MASTER appears silently.

STAIR
Majesty.

STAIR bows low and leaves.

MASTER

Luncheon is served, Ma'am.

There is a new tea sample.

Mr Davies sends it, along with his apologies.

He is apparently taking dancing lessons.

QUEEN ANNE

Do you love me, Willie?

MASTER

Majesty, you are the glorious sun that lightens this poor country's darkness.

QUEEN ANNE

Not just as your queen. As a woman.

MASTER

...

That's not for me to say, Your Majesty.

QUEEN ANNE

I ask you.

Am I... attractive?

The MASTER wonders what on earth to say.

QUEEN ANNE

My body betrays me.

Ravaged by dead babes.

QUEEN ANNE moves towards him. She removes her wig – an elegant train of curls. Places it on his head. Turns him around.

QUEEN ANNE
My darling. My Sarah.

She guides his hand onto her breast. Brings his head to hers and kisses him. She takes his other hand, pulls up her skirts and places his hand on her crotch.

QUEEN ANNE
Remember you love me.

Cut to BLACK.

Scene 4   **Queen Mary's Bedchamber**

Night in the Bedchamber in the Palace of Holyrood.

RAMSAY and GRACE sneak in. She has a cloth bound across her eyes. He guides her, holding a candle.

RAMSAY
Now.
Take it off.

GRACE unbinds the cloth.

GRACE
Mercy...

RAMSAY
Said ah'd give you a palace.

GRACE
How'd ye get us in?!

RAMSAY
Ma cousin's a chambermaid.
She lent me a key.

GRACE
We'll get hanged!

RAMSAY
So quiet is essential.

GRACE
No declaiming yer poetry.

RAMSAY
Isn't it bonnie?
Queen Mary's bedchamber.
Where poor Rizzio was slain by Lord Darnley.

GRACE
Murdered in front of Mary...

RAMSAY
As a pistol was held tae her unborn child...
Ah've got tae write this.

GRACE
Later.

RAMSAY
Leadhills tae Holyrood, eh?
Upward mobility fer poets.

GRACE
What's Leadhills like?

RAMSAY
Ah'm by far its greatest export!
Ah'll take ye when it's warmer.
Ma father would be spitting blood tae see me here.

GRACE
My father was a crofter.
We lived in Angus.

RAMSAY
Cattle country.

GRACE
But he got sick and died.
Came tae Edinburgh with ma mother.
Massive black buildings, towering over.
She got work at the Castle.
But she was awful skinny and Winter took her away.
So ah did her work, in the kitchens.
One day a nobleman followed me up the stair.
He raped me by a window.
But gave me silver and suggested other employment.
The glamour of the brothel beckoned.

RAMSAY
Ye met Macdonald?

GRACE
He was known fer looking after lost lassies.
Never takes a cut.

...
Ah've been here.
Hamilton's the keeper of the Palace.

Beat.

RAMSAY
Let's check out the bed.

GRACE
That's the Queen's bed!

RAMSAY
So it's been well-used!

GRACE is reluctant.

RAMSAY
The finest bed we'll ever see!

GRACE
This room is too sad.

RAMSAY
Let us banish its demons!

GRACE
No, Allan!
There's death here.

RAMSAY

Thought ye wanted a palace?

GRACE

Ah just want tae live.

RAMSAY

Live with me, Grace.
Our country's changing.
We'll get through winter –

GRACE

And then?
Still need to eat.
And our country's being parcelled up fer the English –

RAMSAY

Never happen.
We'll defy them tae the last!

GRACE

Their wealth's too tempting –

RAMSAY

Forget the money!
What cares our land fer coin?!

GRACE

Allan, stop!

RAMSAY

The day's are ours tae seize!

GRACE

Aye, never a dull moment!
That's why ah love ma work!

RAMSAY

Grace –

GRACE

As ye know!
Can ye tell the difference?
Beware lassies, Allan, they wind yer heart about their fingers,
And then smash it just fer kicks.
Now where's yer wit?
An allegory tae inspire?!
Come, let's hear it – ah might just fall in love!

Beat.

RAMSAY

Paris was a shepherd on Mount Ida.
One day, in the fields, three women appeared.
Three goddesses – Athena, Aphrodite and Hera.
They commanded him to choose the most beautiful.
He chose Aphrodite. The only possible choice.

GRACE

How's this –

RAMSAY

When ah first came here there were 3 women sitting outside.
Whores – all advertising their wares.
But one looked me clear in the eye, and only she ah saw.
The only possible choice.
You were waiting for me –
Ever since ah left home and walked all the way here –
Since ma life began you've been waiting –

GRACE

Allan –

RAMSAY

Ah love you Grace – ma heart is so full –
The world has such overwhelming beauty –

GRACE

Allan, ah'm –

RAMSAY

You're my muse –

GRACE

Ah'm a filthy, cheap as they come, ragged street whore!
Where you see beauty, everyone else sees cunt.
What's with these foreign stories?

RAMSAY

It's the Classics —

GRACE

Ah don't speak Latin!

The folk who do, fuck me, carelessly, perversely.

Even you!

Ah've seen yer eyes.

Whether it's gold or kisses,

When yer a whore everyone owns ye.

RAMSAY

Ah belong to you.

GRACE

Then ah release ye!

Ah won't own anyone!

Men only value what they can buy.

Their wives, their estates, their country!

RAMSAY

Our country can't be bought!

GRACE

Money rules.

All politicians gather bribes.

Your hero Queensberry has his price!

RAMSAY

He protects our nation!

GRACE

The Fat Duke's in it fer all he can accumulate!

Nights ah've spent underneath him.

It's no his country he's turned on by,

But pure, old-fashioned greed.

RAMSAY

We must change that!

Like our forefathers we'll sign Declarations, draw up Covenants –

GRACE

Yer as innocent as a virgin.

What power has yer scribbling?

Books burn.

Promises break.

Countries are conquered as maidens are fucked.

It's never poetry and goddesses.

It's dirt, sweat, pain, blood.

Old boys with eager hands and pissy trousers;

Adolescents with desperate pricks and no manners;

Married men, violent with guilt,

All desperate to shove themselves inside you and break something.

And those wee scraps of metal mean they can.

That's yer muse.

There's classes of life, Allan.

And, no matter what you do, you can't move between.
Scribble yer poems, dream!
But don't kid yerself its anything to do with what goes on out there.

She grabs the candle and leaves. RAMSAY is plunged into darkness.

Scene 5   **Queen Anne's Bedchamber**

Kensington Palace, London.

Huge four-poster with crimson drapes. Cushions everywhere. QUEEN ANNE sits up in bed, a simple nightdress covering her. Her hair is down. The MASTER lies sprawled and astonished before her.

MASTER
I adore you.

QUEEN ANNE rises, crosses to a table and pours some tea.

MASTER
Could never tell what's behind those eyes.
You command and I search for a semblance of favour.
A flicker of tenderness.
...
I will be faithful.
Give you whatever you desire.
Future princes. Heirs for your empire.

QUEEN ANNE slowly pulls a brush through her hair.

MASTER
My mother will be so proud.
Always had big ambitions.
We have a place in Suffolk – bit rundown but superb for parties.

The woods we'll wander to our hearts content.
Bridges, shrubbery, lagoons.
Making love in the leaves.
...
I have a sister, Ma'am.
No great beauty.
Her husband speculates.
War. Horses. Amateur dramatics.
We pay off his creditors, but there's only so much one can do.
If there was any way...
Perhaps a knighthood? State pension?
The family would be eternally grateful.
Enfold you in the ever-loving bosom.

He smiles sweetly.

QUEEN ANNE
I have allergies.
Box hedge.
They had to root it all up from Hampton Court, burnt the lot.
The natural world repels me.
Fetch laudanum.

BLACK!

Scene 6   **The Morning After**

Kensington Palace, London.

Reception room of QUEEN ANNE. Doors burst open and the MASTER strides into the room, bearing an enormous bouquet of roses. A changed man! Instead of his lover, another man stands reading a book. ROBERT HARLEY.

HARLEY
I greatly appreciate the thought.
Leave them by the fireplace.
One of the maids will arrange.

The MASTER is affronted. He holds onto his flowers.

MASTER
Where is Her Majesty?

HARLEY
Indisposed.

MASTER
She was in fine spirits last night.
I don't believe you're due to meet Her Majesty until 3 o'clock.

Beat.

HARLEY
You're not required today.

MASTER
I have duties.
State business. Her Majesty's appointments.

HARLEY
All cancelled.

MASTER
Then I shall discuss Her Majesty's new schedule with her.
Please, we have business to attend to...

HARLEY
No.

MASTER
No?

HARLEY
No.

MASTER
I am her diary, Harley!
Nearer her person than a mere politician.

HARLEY
You're relieved from your post.
With immediate effect.

MASTER
Absurd!
Why?!

HARLEY
We do not reason, we simply obey.
Your personal artefacts are in that bag.

The MASTER checks. The bag is there.

MASTER
But... what will I do?

HARLEY
Find other employment.
I'm sure you're capable.

MASTER
This is my life.
I demand to see my Queen.

The MASTER loses it. Rushes the doors.

MASTER
My Queen! My Queen!
Who dares keep us apart??
MAJESTY!!

*He smashes into the doors. Hurts his shoulder – tries again.
Doors do not budge.*

HARLEY
Finished?
There are soldiers at the door.
They will escort you to the gates.

MASTER
I adore her.

HARLEY
As do we all.
But none may presume intimacy of the kind you advocate.

He rings a bell.

HARLEY
You held a position of ultimate trust.
If you breathe a syllable of a state secret,
Or we hear rumours of Her Majesty's habits,
I'll have your throat slit from ear to ear.
Keep your secrets.
And do leave the flowers.
They brighten the place up.

Doors open. Broken, the MASTER leaves court. HARLEY returns to his book.

DEFOE appears.

HARLEY
We need a new Master of Household. Fancy it?

DEFOE
Prefer the perks of my current job.

He nonchalantly takes a seat. Thumbs through HARLEY'S book.

HARLEY
Not one of yours, I'm afraid. Jonathan Swift.

DEFOE
An Irish immigrant with separatist tendencies.

HARLEY
He'll rival you.

DEFOE
A country cleric? I'd eat him alive.
Met the Scots.
Queensberry's a barrel of fun.

HARLEY
He has skill.
Buried beneath chronic alcoholism and rapacious lust.

DEFOE
Stair's the threat. A zealot.
It's believed his mother was a witch.

HARLEY

Anyone who can order Glencoe has his uses.
Fancy a holiday?

DEFOE

Fancy some sun. Winter's atrocious.

HARLEY

I hear it's nice in Edinburgh this time of year.

DEFOE

I don't.

HARLEY

You may call upon all your new friends.
The endgame approaches. About damned time.
Her Majesty anticipates good news.

DEFOE

And you're measuring curtains for the new office.

HARLEY

Once we have a Parliament of Great Britain,
You can have as many tropical holidays as you wish.
How'd you like to pack a knighthood in your luggage?
Or remain here and focus on the writing, put Mr Swift in his
place?

DEFOE

Pay rise?

HARLEY

Don't push your luck.

DEFOE

Bring you back a souvenir?
The Scottish Regalia perhaps?

HARLEY

The satisfaction of duty done will suffice.
You may find the previous Master loitering.
Please remind him of the danger he faces.

DEFOE

What's his trouble?

HARLEY

He's in love with Her Majesty.

DEFOE

Ah! Love!
Warps the finest of men.
Catullus and his prostitute.
"Because that moment I see you, nothing's left of me,
But my tongue is numbed, my voice broken.
And through my helpless limbs fires are raging,
Your voice rings in both ears,
My skins pales like a wisp of straw,
And my eyes are covered by the dark of night."
Ever happen to you, Harley?

HARLEY stares at him. They have never spoken like this before.

DEFOE
Should meet Allan Ramsay.
He'll have you quoting the classics.
Good drinker too.
I'll head north. Stir up trouble.
Serve Her Majesty in these turbulent times.

Throws HARLEY the book.

DEFOE
One for the fire I think.
Ever been to Edinburgh?

HARLEY
No. And I have no inclination to visit.

DEFOE
It's beautiful.
Yeah there's disease, poverty. Winter's appalling.
But the sunlight on the castle. St Giles.
Lightning storms over the Forth.
People are firebrands –

HARLEY
They are fortunate we shan't annihilate them like Ireland.
The Scots retain a great deal.

DEFOE
Imagine it were the other way round?
Scottish Parliament subsuming Westminster?

HARLEY
Don't be absurd.

DEFOE
I'll bring you back some poetry.
After a hard days politicking, you can kick back with Virgil.

HARLEY
Just do your work, Defoe.

He leaves.

DEFOE
Ever your servant, Harley.
Keep the home fires burning.

He takes a look at Swift's book. Peruses.

ACT III

Scene 1   **The Scottish Parliament**

15ᵗʰ January 1707.

Day of the final debate. Present are DUKES OF QUEENSBERRY and HAMILTON, EARLS OF SEAFIELD and STAIR, LORD BELHAVEN.

SEAFIELD
The process of ratification is all but complete.
Tomorrow we must vote.
First, the Duke of Queensberry shall offer us his findings.

QUEENSBERRY addresses the chamber.

QUEENSBERRY
My esteemed Lords. Gentlemen.
Happily, I bring news from the court of our Queen.
Our audience was triumphant.
She is a woman of shrewdness. Vision.
Courteously, she questioned. Patiently, she heeded.
And for days we negotiated. Struggled.
Wiped the sweat from our ravaged brow –

SEAFIELD
I would urge you to get to the point.

QUEENSBERRY

'Tis the belief of my fellow Commissioners,

And our recommendation to this Parliament,

That, for the sake of our nation, and future generations,

Who would eternally regret wasting this precious chance of salvation,

We ratify this Treaty with immediate effect,

And unify these islands.

General clamour. SEAFIELD quietens them.

SEAFIELD

Order!

Since October last year,

Parliament has debated the articles of the Treaty.

All 25 have been accepted.

Tomorrow we vote whether or not to accept the Act of Union,

In its entirety, and formally create Great Britain.

LORDS

Shame!

QUEENSBERRY

No shame in progress, gentlemen.

LORD

Tyranny!

SEAFIELD

We must hear all sides.

So, for the final time, as the foremost opponent of this Treaty,

I call upon his Grace, the Duke of Hamilton to sum up for his faction.

HAMILTON rises to his feet, amid cheers from the pro-independence supporters.

HAMILTON

My lords. Gentleman.

Lord Queensberry. Eternal gratitude.

Steadfast have our Commissioners been in their duty,

Neither swayed by politics, nor seduced by power.

We are thankful our Queen chose so wisely.

QUEENSBERRY bows.

HAMILTON

Cautiously, I tread.

This chamber has witnessed calamitous decisions.

Scotland's turbulent history is beset by crisis.

Our struggle today is no less.

The challenge we face is to our very existence as a nation.

Agreement from his faction.

HAMILTON

Recall 2 years previous.

The English closed their markets to Scottish produce,

Over half our yearly export.

All Scots were declared alien.

Damage to our industries – beef, fishing, wool – incalculable.

Burgeoning colonial opportunities, denied.

Our vulnerability in a trade war, clearly exposed.

Therefore we must carefully consider

Whether to remain alone, or make alliance with a neighbour

–

One with whom we share common bonds of language and monarchy,

And who offers trading opportunities,

Colonial possibilities, and economic security.

Harsh times call for bold decisions.

We in this Parliament must search deep within our breasts

For the courage to make them.

LORD

He's changed his mind?!

BELHAVEN

You propose unity with our greatest rival?

HAMILTON

My lords, whilst fervent nationalism burdens our hearts,

So reason must balance our minds.

LORD

He's selling out!

HAMILTON

No one is selling anything – surely, the point.

BELHAVEN

Do English estates usurp loyalty to your country?

HAMILTON

You dare question my loyalty?

BELHAVEN

Your Grace leads the fight for independence –
In God's name, have you changed your mind??

HAMILTON

Look around you!
This country is on its knees, our coffers bare!
Harvests fail and our exports are annihilated.
English troops muster to invade!
What choice have we left?

LORD

Independence!

HAMILTON

We'll be conquered in a month!
Who shoulders the country's weight?

Us, my lords!
We must safeguard our nation.

Uproar!

BELHAVEN
We are deluded!
England is saddled by great debt!
Her Parliament is corrupted by Tory and Whig factions,
Who care only for their county estates!
How does this Treaty protect Scotland?!

QUEENSBERRY
Scotland's best interests are at its heart.
Preserved are the Church, legal and education systems.
Royal Burghs shall have continuation –

BELHAVEN
But not our Parliament?

STAIR
His lordship's place may await at the new Parliament of
Great Britain?
Or perhaps the English are tragically unaware of Lord
Belhaven's worth?!

BELHAVEN
But not unaware of your worth, Lord Stair?
How might you profit from this treaty?

STAIR

We all profit!

The English offer us £398,085 and 10 shillings,

As compensation for the Darien disaster,

Which, need I remind this chamber, was led by you, sir!

BELHAVEN

I take no lectures from the architect of Glencoe!

Your troops butchered a community!

STAIR

You lost Scotland's liquid assets!

BELHAVEN

Slaughtered children!

STAIR

Bankruptcy!

— Amidst noise, SEAFIELD struggles for control —

SEAFIELD

ORDER!

My lords!

Parliament will not dissolve into chaos!

BELHAVEN

I have not received answers!

SEAFIELD

Time has passed for debate.

This day's business is concluded. Tomorrow we vote!

Scene 2   **The Saltyre**

Edinburgh.

The evening pub is deserted but for ALLAN RAMSAY. He's a wreck, barely survived the winter. He writes at his table, drinking.

A figure appears from shadow. DEFOE.

DEFOE
Greetings Master Ramsay!
Looking for nobility, but I'll settle for poets!
Barely recognise you.
Macdonald says you drink 'til he throws you out.
Spouting poetry, fighting.
The whores fuck you out of pity.
Just like a proper writer.
You look as wretched as your country.
Edinburgh's changed since last I visited.
Riots by the Parliament.

RAMSAY
Keep yer head down.
The mob will destroy anything English they can find.

DEFOE
If you all agree.
Your Scots rabble is the worst of its kind,
For every 1 in favour there's 99 against.

Where's your lover? The whore?

...

Captured your heart, didn't she?

RAMSAY
She was right about you.

DEFOE
Whores have sharp instincts.

RAMSAY
English spy –

DEFOE
Go carefully, Allan –

RAMSAY
That's how a writer commands nobility –

DEFOE
Games and jests –

RAMSAY
High stakes –

DEFOE
Why play for anything less?
Kings and nations come and go.

RAMSAY

And spies.

DEFOE

And Parliaments.
Yours commits national suicide.
Unifying your country with England.
We'll be brother-citizens.
One monarch. One Parliament.
Albion, Caledonia, Hibernia.
Merry old Britannia.
Shouldn't reveal this to a poet.
He'll grow all revolutionary.
It's been a treat, Ramsay.
Keep scribbling.
You've a singular talent.

DEFOE disappears.

RAMSAY

Macdonald! *Macdonald!*

MACDONALD brings him a bottle of wine.

MACDONALD

When you gonnae pay me?
Your credit would bankrupt a nation.
There's no food. Traders empty-handed.
...
Like a storm sitting there.

Raining all over my tables, scaring customers.
"Who's the bampot in the corner?"
"Covered in ink, talking to himself, screaming drunk?"
Yer a good customer Allan – actually in sales terms yer the best, but...
Of all the folk drinking themselves to death,
Never seen anyone as committed as you.
...
What you writing?
What are these for?

RAMSAY ignores. MACDONALD picks up a book.

MACDONALD
"Seneca."
You've read all these?

RAMSAY nods.

MACDONALD
Why?
What've they to do with us?
Wee kids starving.
Whores dying.
Favour went yesterday.
Rotted by disease from the core out.
Her face was the only thing untouched.
Scotland's decaying, Ramsay.
The tide reveals our blackened shore.
And all the heroes in your books won't be saving us.

MACDONALD pours himself wine.

MACDONALD
There's a valley, up west, behind the mist.
The Sisters tower over.
Water runs down like tears and the wind whistles through.
No, not whistles. Nothing would now.
In Spring the ground thaws.
Anemones and violets push through, ignoring the sadness.
Everything forgets as nature winds her cycle.
But these flowers pray for winter's departure,
Cos when the snow leaves, maybe it'll melt the deed away,
Wash it down the pass and into Rannoch Moor,
Seeping back to the soil we all come from.
But blood cries out.
You wash away the red, but the stains never leave.
When you've seen the children lying in the snow...

MACDONALD takes a drink.

RAMSAY
More wine, Macdonald.

RAMSAY flings a full purse on the table.

MACDONALD
Lay in the heather, watching.
High up the mountain, looking down the whole valley.
Saw the militia sweeping up and down.
Gunfire, horses, sounds of soldiers.

When our families screamed, we watched.
When they burned our crofts, we watched.
Only when dark came, did we move.
Bodies strewed the valley.
Few dozen, not a battlefield.
Wee ones and old ones tangled together.
Now just bodies.
Mort Ghlinne Comhann.

Door swings open.

GRACE stands there. She is a mess. RAMSAY registers.

GRACE
Ah need you.
How much money d'you have?
...
Money, Ramsay.

RAMSAY
Where've you been?
Let me feed you.

GRACE doesn't move.

GRACE
Ye got any?

RAMSAY
Why?

GRACE

Ah need tae get rid of it.
Nearly too late.

RAMSAY

Is it...
Did ah...?

GRACE

It's not cheap.
But ah know you've got funds.

RAMSAY

Where will you go?

GRACE

There's a woman who does it.
Looks after us lassies.
Pulls em out clean and whole like little lambs.

RAMSAY picks up his bag of coin.

RAMSAY

Show me.

GRACE leaves. RAMSAY follows, bringing a cloak.

Scene 3   **The Abortion House**

Edinburgh.

A grim house, down a dark close. Rain spatters buildings.
Wind gusts.

GRACE and RAMSAY appear. GRACE wears his cloak.

RAMSAY
Don't go in.
Have the child.
Ah'll take care of you both.
Ah'll make it work – ma writing...

GRACE goes to the door. Bangs on it.

GRACE
Ever think of killing yerself just tae see what it's like?

RAMSAY
... Yes.

GRACE
Why don't you?

She goes in. Door shuts with the finality of a tomb

RAMSAY waits. Storm grows worse. Wind whips through the
close.

MACDONALD races in, breathing hard.

MACDONALD
Allan, come away!
This place is cursed!

RAMSAY
Grace is in there!

MACDONALD
Let her go!
There's mobs on the streets!
They're out for blood!
Parliament betrays us!
Word is they're annulling themselves.

*A gut-wrenching cry from inside. RAMSAY stares at the house
– he wrenches the door open, rushes in…*

Scene 4   **Inside the House**

RAMSAY races down stairs, down and down into the darkness...

A tiny room. In the centre is a table. On the table lies GRACE, on her back. Still wearing her dress, she's covered in blood. RAMSAY moves to her.

GRACE
Allan...

RAMSAY
Aye, ah'm here, ah'm here.
Did it... has she...

GRACE
Aye she did. She took it.
Ah'm sorry.

GRACE tries to sit up –

RAMSAY
No. No –

GRACE
Am ah a state?

RAMSAY
You're beautiful...
And you'll be grand.

GRACE
Ah'd have had it.
But this wasn't ours.
Our child will be bonnie.
He'll want fer nothing.
And his country will love him.
It's very cold.

RAMSAY
Ah'll take you out of here.

GRACE
Allan, ah'm scared –

RAMSAY
You're not going –

GRACE
Ah've done wicked things – ah'm for the fire –

RAMSAY
No –

GRACE
They're coming for me.
Burning hands – pulling – ah'm not strong enough...

RAMSAY holds her. She's fading fast.

GRACE
That man. The Roman who loved a whore.

RAMSAY
Catullus.

GRACE
"Let us live, my darling, let us love…"

RAMSAY
"And all the words of the old, and so moral,
May they be worth less than nothing to us.
Suns may set, and suns may rise again…"

GRACE
You're writing?

RAMSAY
A story about Paris.

GRACE
He had eyes for only one.

She struggles to hand him something. A note.

GRACE
Here.
Keep it safe.

She's fading and he knows it.

RAMSAY
Ah wrote you letters.
To get everything down before ah lost it.
But they stop at the same place.
Where ah see you for the last time.
Wrap myself in sheets you lay in.
Scent of your hair.
Sweat of what we'd done.
Piled up our sheets, paper, poems, everything,
And ah burnt the lot.
You're right.
Pain and tears and blood.
We accept our lot and we struggle on.
But if we find something that ignites our soul,
That rewards our existence,
We hold it with all the strength God gave us.
We hold on. We hold on.

She's gone.

RAMSAY
"Suns may set, and suns may rise again,
But when our brief light has set,
Night is one long everlasting sleep."

He opens up the note. It's the list of lords receiving money.
DEFOE's list.
RAMSAY holds GRACE in the darkness.

217

Scene 5   Grassmarket

MACDONALD addresses the mob.

MACDONALD
People of Scotland!
Listen tae me!
We've been betrayed.
Up there they write our nation out of existence!
Parliament turns against its own people!
As they did in Glencoe!

VOICE
Shame!

MACDONALD
Folk starving in the streets!
Whilst *they* only know avarice!
Glutted by privilege, gorging on our graft, our suffering –
Why, in this country's name, should we stand it any longer??

VOICE
He's right!

MACDONALD
These grandees must heed us!
Or we'll raze Parliament to the ground!

VOICE
Tae the ground!

MACDONALD
Bring torches!
We'll light such fires that put yon London blaze tae shame!

MACDONALD and mob head for the Parliament...

Scene 6 Parliament Square

SERGEANT CAMPBELL guards the Parliament building. He's armed.

RAMSAY stares up at the Parliament. He takes the note out his pocket.

RAMSAY
Ah must enter.
Parliament decides our future.
The men we trust tae protect us.

SERGEANT
The doors are closed.

RAMSAY
Ah bring a message for Lord Belhaven.
Forgot to give him my receipt.
Three new wigs, including the one he wears.
Should Parliament pass the Act of Union,
Ah might never see him again, and ah'd like the credit settled.

SERGEANT
Stand back!

He raises his weapon –

RAMSAY

Listen.

Ah've a list.

A list of Scots who took English money for their vote.

They were bribed!

SERGEANT

Still not getting in.

RAMSAY

They're selling our country!

What's yer name?

SERGEANT

Sergeant Campbell.

Beat.

RAMSAY

Campbell? Argyll's militia?

It's sewn up. Stair protects Parliament so he can betray it.

RAMSAY spits on the ground at the SERGEANT'S feet.

RAMSAY

That's for yer bastard devil Stair!

Oh pity yer friends when they learn who you protect!

Campbells are cursed for all time –

Soldiers who butchered innocents in the snow!
Slept in their homes and then hacked them to death!
Did ye waste musket balls? Or just use bayonets?

SERGEANT
Keep back!!

RAMSAY
There's a mob charging up the Royal Mile, a thousand strong.
They'll crush you, storm Parliament and burn it tae the ground!
My Macdonald barman leads them —
If ah cry "Campbell" they'll come like deerhounds, to avenge the slain.
Winter corpses — burns black with blood —
Screams of the slaughtered — whistling through yer mind...
CAMPBELL!!

GUARD
No!!

RAMSAY
Take this inside!
Take it to Lord Belhaven.
I beg you.

SERGEANT CAMPBELL takes the note...

Scene 7　　　　　**The Scottish Parliament**

16ᵗʰ January, 1707.

Chaos – lords of each faction argue. Through the commotion, a bell rings. The EARL OF SEAFIELD rings the great session bell. Chaos subsides a little –

SEAFIELD
The hour is upon us.
The votes have been counted.
I announce the results.

Clamour persists.

SEAFIELD
Order!
The results of the vote proposing the Treaty of the Act of Union.
The Ayes 110.
The Noes 67.
The Abstentions –

Uproar. Condemnation and jubilation.

LORDS
Victory!

BELHAVEN
SHAME!
Shame on this chamber!

STAIR
Do you challenge democracy, Lord Belhaven?

BELHAVEN
When bought by foreign gold, yes!

STAIR
What can you be alleging?

BELHAVEN
This country has been sold to her most devout enemy!

STAIR
Treason, my lords – to doubt the integrity of this chamber –

BELHAVEN
I do not doubt, I openly question it!

SEAFIELD
You forget yourself, Belhaven!
No parliamentarian, however rash, is above the law.
You shall be arrested – guards!

BELHAVEN holds up the note.

BELHAVEN

Treason's proof.

A list of those paid off, my Lord.

Names on the left. Bribes on the right.

STAIR

Scandalous!

BELHAVEN

I fully agree, Lord Stair.

The Dukes of Atholl and Argyle receive £1200 between them
—

SEAFIELD

I will not permit —

BELHAVEN

Whereas our Lord Chancellor receives a mere £490.

Is that the pathetic price of his vote?!

Silence.

BELHAVEN

This note lists 32 men of this country

Who accepted payment from England —

STAIR

For expenses incurred in bringing this Treaty to pass —

BELHAVEN

And who benefits the most?

Our beloved Duke of Queensberry.

He receives £12,325, for selling his country into slavery.

Bought and sold, my lords! Bought and sold for foreign gold!

SEAFIELD

Order! Order!

BELHAVEN

Around me are gathered the great of our country.

Friends, rivals, kith and kin.

But we have notable absentees!

Our gracious Duke of Hamilton, saviour of independence,

Misses this crucial vote, citing toothache,

Whilst his comrades enter into pact with the Westminster
Devil!

STAIR

Baseless accusations!

BELHAVEN

I see cowards struggling to hide bribes and embarrassment.

And I see an independent kingdom freely giving up

That which all the world has been fighting for, to wit:

The right to manage her own affairs by herself,

Without the counsel of any other –

SEAFIELD

She has given up, Lord Belhaven. The votes cannot be recast.

BELHAVEN

I see men whose ancestors fought with the Bruce,
Tamely surrender hard-gotten freedoms –

STAIR

By God you'll swing for this!

BELHAVEN

But above all, I see our ancient mother Caledonia,
Like Caesar sitting in the midst of our Senate,
Ruefully looking about her, covering herself with her royal garment,
Attending the fatal blow and breathing out her last!

Cheers and boos from both sides respectively.

SEAFIELD

This is a Parliament, Lord Belhaven, not a common stage.
If there are legal matters to address, let the courts decide.

BELHAVEN tries to interrupt –

SEAFIELD
ENOUGH!
We abide by parliamentary rules!
Our forefathers died for the democracy we enjoy –

BELHAVEN

For shame, sir!

SEAFIELD

You shame the integrity of this parliament!

BELHAVEN

You dishonour the role of Chancellor!

STAIR

YOU LOST, BELHAVEN!!
You lost the vote! Step aside!

BELHAVEN

Gladly – no longer will I consort with traitors.
We will be judged, lords!
Scotland has been betrayed by centuries of feuding.
And the members of this honour-soiled chamber
Can now add their names to that despised scroll.
Where stands our loyalty? Where our national pride?
This assembly is only fit for the slaves who've sold it.

He leaves. Parliamentary chaos resumes –

SEAFIELD

Order!
In the name of Her Majesty, this chamber will come to order!

Parliament comes close to an order.

SEAFIELD

We are a civilised chamber, not a barbarian horde.

The votes have been counted and the motion carried.

The ink dries on the Parliamentary scroll,

As clerks record our actions for posterity.

A new chapter begins, my lords.

A glorious opportunity to advance our country,

In harmony with our great sister nation England,

Towards a brighter dawn.

It is the ruling of this Parliament that the proposed Act of Union

Is passed into law, and our express command it is carried out forthwith.

Let it be set down in the records that the margin of victory was significant.

I believe it necessary for establishing the lasting peace,

Happiness and prosperity of both nations.

SEAFIELD touches the document with his staff.

SEAFIELD

And there's the end of that old song.

BLACK.

Scene 8   **Kensington Palace**

4th March, 1707.

QUEEN ANNE stands, viewing her figure in a full-length mirror. Her hair is down. She slowly puts on her crown.

4th March, 1707.

ROBERT HARLEY addresses the English Parliament at Westminster.

HARLEY
My fellow Members of Parliament.
I spy a new dawn.
God blesses this land, and our majestic sovereign.
Since October, our sister parliament in Edinburgh has been in session.
Bravely have our Queen's Commissioners there battled for Union.
After toil, trial, tears and tribulation, success has finally come.
The Act of Union has been passed.
I read directly from the preface of the Act,
Dated the 16th day of January, Seventeen Hundred and Seven.

"The two kingdoms of Scotland and England shall,
Upon the 1st day of May next ensuing the date hereof, and for ever after,
Be united into one kingdom by the name of Great Britain,
And the ensigns armorial of the said United Kingdom
Be such as Her Majesty shall appoint,
And the crosses of St Andrew and St George be conjoined
In such manner as her Majesty shall think fit,

And used in all flags, banners, standards and ensigns, both at sea and land..."

It continues for a further 25 articles, which I leave you to read leisurely.

Both countries will share one monarchy, the same succession,

And a new single parliament, here at Westminster.

Some Scots institutions shall continue,

Although Westminster shall retain final say.

A country has been gained.

Peace brought.

Our glorious monarch, Her Majesty, Queen Anne, may God defend her,

Has finally sealed the legacy of her ancestor James I –

A united island.

Let church bells ring out the glad tidings.

And may we, who strive tirelessly for our country's good,

Work with courage and fortitude to bring this glorious new Parliament into being.

He bows. Massive cheers ring around the House of Commons, as we move to –

Scene 10   **The Nor Loch**

25ᵗʰ March, 1707.

ALLAN RAMSAY stands beside Edinburgh's Nor Loch.

RAMSAY

History is always *written*.
Our Scottish Parliament meets for the last time,
Scrawling itself out of existence.
In Leith our harbour readies for English warships.
400 miles south the Queen negotiates new wars –
The clerks documenting all.
Details, footnotes, moments becoming history.
And us, Grace, something of us will last.
The shadow of a glimmer of something once begun.

RAMSAY writes a note for Grace.

RAMSAY

Went back to that house, looking for you.
Not a trace.
Not even blood on the stones.
The woman swore she didn't know.
One of hundreds she's fixed.
Ah write everything now.
You pervade all.

He lets the note fall into the Nor Loch.

RAMSAY

There will come a time, you will see,
Hearts will be 'mended and our country free.
Writers spy, lords corrupt,
Poets dream of love.
The good we're made of never passes,
It merely recalibrates, then surpasses,
Even God himself above.
Future echoes fall with rain,
Gently cradling our country's pain.
Words fade, love letters drown,
Gathering in a forlorn sea,
And now Grace, my one true Grace,
Ah must finally let you be.

*His note floats in the water. It's not alone. There's thousands
of them. All slowly turning to soggy nothing in the rain.*

FINAL BLACKOUT.